Boy Guerrilla

Boy Guerrilla

The World War II Metro Manila Serenader

Rudy de Lara, with Bob Fancher

Writer's Showcase
presented by *Writer's Digest*
San Jose   New York   Lincoln   Shanghai

Boy Guerrilla
The World War II Metro Manila Serenader

All Rights Reserved © 2000 by Rudy de Lara

No part of this book may be reproduced or transmitted in any form or by any means, graphic, electronic, or mechanical, including photocopying, recording, taping, or by any information storage retrieval system, without the permission in writing from the publisher.

Writer's Showcase
presented by *Writer's Digest*
an imprint of iUniverse.com, Inc.

For information address:
iUniverse.com, Inc.
5220 S 16th, Ste. 200
Lincoln, NE 68512
www.iuniverse.com

ISBN: 0-595-14806-9

Printed in the United States of America

*To my parents and family,
who gave me life; and for the benefit
of those people in Don Galo to whom
life has not offered its easier paths.*

Contents

Chapter One	Tough Kid in Paradise	1
Chapter Two	History of a Pro-American	24
Chapter Three	Boy Guerrilla in Love	35
Chapter Four	Liberation	56
Chapter Five	Kidnapped	76
Chapter Six	Charged with Murder	93
Chapter Seven	When Stella Died	109
Chapter Eight	On Trial	115
Chapter Nine	Clinging to a Dream, Alone	120
Chapter Ten	A Student in America	128
Chapter Eleven	Married, then Not	138
Chapter Twelve	Finding Myself	149
Epilogue	My Life	158
About the Author		167

Chapter One

Tough Kid in Paradise

I have passed my three-score-and-ten. I have, in times past, been a guerrilla fighter and a gambler. I have been kidnapped and tried for murder. I have driven fast cars and danced through blissful nights, known many women, loved some, and married two. I have fathered five children, who live successfully and well. I have made efforts, though too small, to give care for the poor of my native land—a land from which I have been exiled, not by politics but by memories too strong to bear, memories of Stella. Though I loved her in life only a short while, since she died she has shaped everything I have been.

Perhaps you think I exaggerate, that I have grown nostalgic. Come with me, then, as I tell you the story of my life, and see whether this child-woman, so long dead, has not occupied—haunted—everything I have been.

Though she lived across the road from the time I was a child, Stella played no role in my life until I was about eighteen. That was shortly after the Philippines fell to the Japanese in World War II and I had joined the underground resistance. My childhood did not foretell how my life would go. My childhood was idyllic.

To start with, I am, by birth, Filipino. No place on Earth surpasses the Philippines in physical beauty. About 4,000 miles west of Hawaii and 700 miles south of China, the 7,000 islands that make up the country suffer no rivals in tropical splendor. Because our islands lie far from other lands, many unique animals and flowers developed there. Biologists say we have over 10,000 kinds of plants, including nearly a thousand species of orchids, covering the dramatic mountains and broad valleys. We have about six hundred species of animals. Of course, I never counted them. I give you the numbers so you can have some idea of the amazing array in which I grew up. Imagine the richest variety of tropical plants and animals, then allow for many types unique to our islands, and you have some idea of the Philippines. Since I was born in 1924, the Philippines had suffered few ravages of modern life when I knew it best. It was just beautiful.

You probably know that the Philippines suffers a terrible divide between the very wealthy few and everyone else. A few dozen families control most of the economy (and politics, for that matter). This goes back to the time of the Spaniards, who owned and occupied the Philippines for over three hundred years. I shall say more about that later. What I want you to understand now, though, is that this terrible divide between rich and poor is not so black-and-white as you think. Far below the filthy-rich oligarchy, you find a class of people far less wealthy but, compared to most people, fairly well-to-do. These are hard-working local merchants and businessmen, people who do not hold huge estates or export great amounts of goods, but who cater to the local population and manage their affairs shrewdly. My father was one of those.

My father provided for us one of the finest lives in our barrio. He had a fish farm, a rice farm, and a farm for vegetables and chickens. He made and sold salt, and he owned a bakery. At various times he owned a night club, a rattan furniture factory, a bowling alley, a *sabongan* (cock-fighting arena), and a concrete block manufacturing company. By American standards, our way of living was not very high, but by Filipino standards, we were very well off.

Our family lived in the town of Paranaque, a few miles south of Manila—by the time World War II started, our little town was considered part of Metro Manila. The town of Paranaque was made up of six barrios. When Ferdinand Marcos became President, years after he defended me against murder charges, he decided we should no longer use the Spanish term "barrio," so he said we should call barrios "*barangay*," instead. *Barangay* was the name of the type of boat our earliest ancestors used to come to the Philippines from the Malay kingdom. I still say "barrio," simply because that is how I had thought of our little neighborhoods for decades before Marcos in his "wisdom" changed the name.

When I was born, our barrio, Don Galo, contained no paved roads. It had several "big" twenty-foot-wide dirt roads and many eight-foot-wide side roads. These side roads were wide enough for the *caratelas*—two-wheeled carts drawn by horses, used to transport both people and goods—to pass. Around 1936, the main thoroughfare into Manila was paved. We lived on one of the "big" roads. Altogether, these roads cut Don Galo into maybe seventy or eighty square blocks, each two or three acres in size. Most blocks contained about four houses, though many had but one or two. Every little block was rich with fruit trees and flowering trees—the tall tamarinds, the acacias, and many others. You could walk from the south end of Don Galo to the north end in less than fifteen minutes and from east to west in about ten minutes.

Don Galo was surrounded by fields and jungles, with water on three sides. On the west side was the Manila Bay on the South China Sea, where the water was blue-green and salty and the sunsets are the most beautiful in the world. Fine gray sand there makes lovely beaches, where we all loved to stroll and picnic and gather in the evenings. At the south end of Don

Galo the Paranaque River—which is not really a river but a tidal estuary, an inland extension of the ocean—comes from the Manila Bay. The river turns north, running up the east side of Don Galo. The water was very clean.

The population of Don Galo was about 500 back then. We were really a seaside agrarian village. Most of our people fished or farmed. Paranaque provided much of the fresh seafood for Manila. There were also many "*kutseros*," people making a living by driving the *caratelas*. A few of our people were employed by the government in Manila, and they all wore white suits. There were a few barber shops and a few small "*sari-sari*" shops—convenience stores similar to "7-11" but much smaller, with fewer goods for sale. There were no gasoline stations in the whole town of Paranaque, but we had four blacksmiths in our barrio. That makes sense, for we only had two cars in Don Galo but many *caratelas*.

When I was growing up, about ninety percent of the homes were small, wood-frame houses with corrugated steel roofing. The rest of the houses were made of bamboo, with nipa roofs. All the houses were earthquake-proof, but the bamboo houses had to be specially braced against storms and high wind. Almost all the bamboo homes were replaced with wooden homes before World War II. We had a few earthquakes of different intensities each year, and we had our share of storms and typhoons. Such is the price of tropical splendor.

Our barrio suffered little crime. We never locked our doors, even at night, though we had dead bolts and door keys. Our municipal jail was always empty.

By the time I was about three years old, my father had started taking me for long walks on the beach before sunrise. In the dry season, we walked almost every morning; even in the rainy season, we would walk whenever weather permitted. During our walks, he taught me arithmetic and other subjects. By age four, I could even do multiplication and division orally. My father also told me stories and taught me a lot of history—I will tell you more about that in the next chapter. We usually ended up eating breakfast at the small café in the block across from our house. I would have the kinds of steamed native foods usually eaten for snacks, and I loved having them for breakfast after a tiring walk. These morning walks were wonderful. If I had a cold or cough, the salty, fresh, early-morning air cured my ailment. Whether I was sick or not, I learned so much and enjoyed being with my father.

Some times he took me to the Ibayo Bridge across the Paranaque River, which he had built for the town, and proudly explained how it was built. The deck was laminated wood with asphaltic concrete topping, supported by concrete beams and columns that rested on wood-pile foundations. I did not understood at the time what he was explaining, but I was very impressed. The bridge still stands. He was not even an engineer, but he was very smart and knew how to find out what needed to be done.

My father also told me the story of our family name, "de Lara." In 1734, while the Philippines was part of the Spanish Empire, the king of Spain sent Sabiniano Manrique de Lara, a young lawyer, to be Governor General. He brought his beautiful, 21-year-old wife with him. He was tall—6'6", which was unusual for a Spaniard—and very handsome. He was very slim, with dark hair and blue eyes. He was only in his early thirties, and women from all walks of life were after him. After a number of years of trying, his wife had not been able to bear him children. He turned to socializing and womanizing. His Filipina mistress bore him seven sons. Eventually he became quite dissolute, an obese, ill-kempt alcoholic. He completely stopped ruling the country, leaving it to the unchallenged rule of the church. The king and the Council of the Indies in Madrid ordered him to come home. He tried to take the seven boys with him, but the Council forbade it. He tried all legal means, to no avail. Two of the boys later joined their father and his wife, who became their adoptive mother, in Barcelona. The rest of the brothers stayed in the island, married, and melded with the natives.

My father was a descendant of the governor. Even today, the story of the seven de Lara brothers remains one of the great folk legends of the Philippines. A number of books have been written about it, and a couple of motion pictures made. My father and the long line of the de Laras were very proud of the "de Lara" name.

Governor General de Lara accomplished something that will be long remembered. He was responsible for building the famous walled city of Manila, "Intramuros." I was but a small child when my father took me to Intramuros, showing me the plaque giving credit to our ancestor.

Besides our morning walks, many times my father took me quail hunting, on the way to and around his farms in the fields of Paranaque. For him, these were both business and pleasure trips, as he would talk to his caretakers and check on his enterprises. He carried a 20 gauge, double-barreled shotgun for hunting—which, incidentally, he also fired in the air during many a New Year's Eve.

Amang also took me a few times to his salt beds and explained how salt was made and how fish were raised. During the six months of the rainy season, he used his ponds to raise fish. During the dry season, he used them to make salt. I thought that was very smart.

When I was five years old, my father began taking me to his salt warehouse, where his workers filled orders from wholesale buyers. I helped count the number of 40 kilo bags carried from the warehouse to the large boats of the buyers on the shoulders of strong men. I remember that one day a carrier fell and broke his knee. Carriers worked for the buyer, not my father. They had no health insurance or money to pay for the doctor. My father gave the man some money. My father explained that the carriers earned the lowest wage, and without help from him the poor man could not get care.

I innocently asked why those men did not just get easier jobs with more pay. My father explained that when those men were young, there were no public schools, for the Spanish had not wanted the common people to become educated. Since those men had come from poor families, they had had to work since they were boys like me. I was at that time about to enter the public schools provided by the Americans. To this day I remember the man who broke his knee with little pay.

I stopped going with my father for the early morning walks, quail hunting, and trips to his salt-making place around the time I was in the fourth grade. I became interested in girls and cars. I began spending more time with my school friends. I got involved in sports and, sad to say, gambling. Though my father and I never again spent so much time together, those early years gave me great gifts. My father remains to this day my hero and role model.

We called our mother "Inang". She preferred to be called that way. Some mothers liked to be called "Nanay," while others preferred to be called "Mamá," with the accent on the second syllable. Although we do not have a rigid "class system" in the Philippines like in India, people are clearly, if informally, classified as poor, average, or rich. If you are poor or average, you would normally call your mother "Inang" or "Nanay," and that would be fine. Addressing your mother as "Mamá" signifies a higher social class or financial standing. If you are not wealthy and you call your mother "Mamá," you cross an invisible line, pretending to be what you are not. People will just look down on you for your pretense. There are no monetary fines but the penalty is harder to take than just paying a fine.

I am referring to what went on in the Tagalog-speaking areas surrounding the city of Manila when I was a boy. In Manila, things were different. "Anything goes" would have been true there, because most people came to Manila from the provinces and nobody really knew or cared if you are rich or poor so long as you did not cause problems. If you lived in Manila, you could call your mother "Mamá" even if you ate only once a day. Nobody would care. Siblings called their parents by the first name and that was O.K.

In our town of Paranaque, though, everybody knew everybody. If we were not cousins, we were probably friends. If we were not friends, chances were that we were enemies—political enemies, that is—and we therefore knew each other very well. If you called your mother "Mamá" and your father was a poor fisherman or a poor farmer or a jobless person, people would ridicule you. There are, of course, wealthy farmers and wealthy fishermen. Our family could probably have called our mother "Mamá" and no one would have thought ill of us; but my mother did not want that.

Inang's real name was Felisa Hernandez. She was the youngest daughter of Francisco and Ana Hernandez. Inang was about twenty years younger than her eldest sister. Her only brother, Ciano, was the Chief of Police in Paranaque.

The Hernandez family were, for generations, very prominent and wealthy in Paranaque; but my mother's grandparents lost their fortune in the mid-nineteenth century, when they became enemies of the church. Spanish colonial officials came to the Philippines, stayed long enough to make their fortunes, and returned to Spain. It was quite different with the friars. In the Philippines, they enjoyed more wealth and unchecked power than they had in Spain. They owned vast tracts of lands and worked the peasants very hard. To be fair, they were also obsessed with their mission to make the Philippines a Catholic country and—with great success—dedicated their lives to it. They ruled the country without much constraint, if any, from the Governor General or his officials, using God to demand absolute, blind loyalty to the church and their own policies. If the natives defied their authority, which my great grandparents had chosen to do, they became enemies of the church. The church called in the colonial officials, who took whatever you had, giving it to the church—with a healthy split for themselves. So my mother, in spite of her distinguished family, grew up poor.

My mother was so beautiful. She had very light skin, with freckles on her cheeks and arms. Her eyes were not brown or hazel in color but closer to green. She had a more Spanish complexion than anyone else in our family. When I was about five or six years old, I asked her repeatedly why her skin color was so light, like the Americans. Why was I very dark and she was very white? Her response was always the same: "God gave it to me, but it does not really matter. What really matters is what's inside us. If a person is beautiful inside, that is better than just having fair skin."

She was not only beautiful, but she was also a good singer and dancer. She did those for the church. Unlike my father, who only went to church once a year (on Three Kings Day, January 6, his birthday—he was named for one of the kings, Melchor), she was very religious and went to church almost every day. When she was a girl, every year on the Day of Resurrection, she danced "Batti" in the procession around Paranaque. After she married, she continued teaching the dance until her later years.

She was a teenager when she fell in love with my father, who was a widower, more than fifteen years her senior, with a young daughter. He was already doing well at making salt and raising fish for a living, and he was an elected official, a town councilman in Paranaque.

She had a full-time job at home. She raised five children of her own, in addition to three other sons who died at early ages. She took in many poor relatives. When I was about six years old, our family included about twelve people. There were later years when we were more. There were always plenty of mouths to feed, and my mother enjoyed watching us eat her delicious cooking. She grew up poor, and now that she could afford it, she enjoyed having big company. We really did not live extravagantly; we just had plenty of poor relatives.

Inang took care of us personally from birth until we could do things on our own. For instance, she bought all my clothes and shampooed my hair at least once a week until I was four or five years old. I hated being shampooed, for the shampoo, made from the native bark called "gugu," was very foamy and irritated my eyes very strongly. I would always disappear when it was my turn to be tortured, after she was done with my sister. There was plenty of shouting, scolding, screaming, and crying during the hair washing sessions. I later found out that "gugu" had been used for hundred of years and was very effective in getting rid of lice and dandruff.

Inang went to market, a ten minute walk, every morning, with the company of one of our maids to carry the heavy baskets. We did not have supermarkets like those in America. There was only one central market, called "*palenke*" in Tagalog, our native language. Open from 6 a.m. to 3 p.m.

each day, it was the noisiest place in town. The *palenke* was a big open structure, consisting of a corrugated, galvanized iron roof supported by free-standing rectangular concrete columns, and a solid concrete floor. The municipal government owned it, and each vendor paid a fee at the end of the day. All vendors vacated the place in the afternoon so it could be cleaned.

Each vendor had a permanent location at a rectangular, concrete table. At two or three tables, vendors sold just fresh pork, and at two tables they sold fresh meat. There were tables for fish and shellfish. Coops of squawking chickens, to be sold alive, were piled around one table, and at a table near that one, a man made his money just killing and dressing the chickens. There was no refrigeration, so pork and meat were all fresh. In a separate small building at the back, called "*matadera*," pigs and cows were slaughtered. There were pots and pans and all kinds of locally-made baskets for sale. There were tables just for fruits and vegetables, and others laden with all kinds of native sweets. At the back was a large toilet—I do not remember whether it was "coed," but I only remember the one huge restroom.

For about three months each rainy season, Inang was in charge of selling the fish from Amang's fish pond. Since no one had refrigeration, all the fish had to be sold fresh. Inang would make her rounds to about ten fishmongers in the market and around town. She would also give our neighbors and relatives *regalos* (presents) during the catching period. Those were shrimps, crabs, and other fish species that were not for sale, just for our own consumption and for sharing. During this three months of harvesting, we had seafood several times a day, prepared many different ways.

Inang worked very hard in the morning. In the afternoon, she played cards and also a game similar to bingo. In late afternoon, dinner had to be prepared under her supervision.

Going to the movies was her weakness. She went at least two times and sometimes three times a week. She loved to see those tear-jerker movies that made her cry. Most Filipino stories would make you cry. Later, when television arrived, she still went to the movies occasionally. Her favorite attire was "*baro at saya*" (Filipina native blouse and skirt), which she wore every day, to a very stunning effect.

My family's first house, where my brothers and sisters and I were all born, was built shortly after my parents were married in 1915. It was a two-story wooden house with corrugated roofing. On the upper floor, we had two bedrooms, a large living room, a dining room and a kitchen. On the ground floor, we had a small kitchen, a tiny garage, and two small, all-purpose rooms. My father had an area where he stored his tools and junk. I still remember seeing food cooking in clay pots on the wood-burning stoves of that first house.

We did not have running water when I was very young. Our house had a steel tank where rain water was deposited from the roof. We used this water for cooking and, after boiling, for drinking. We used water from the well in our back yard for everything else. Our neighbors always came to us for free water, since few people had wells. My father liked to help those without wells, but giving away water also kept our well fresh and clean. We had a toilet on the ground floor, where we also took our baths. Don Galo finally got running water just about the time our main road to Manila was paved.

Our family always had more than enough food on the table, and we were never hungry. Our small rice farm supplied more than enough for our staple food. We had rolls for breakfast from father's bakery, fish from his pond, and chicken and fruits from his farm. We ate three square meals a day and snacks in mid-morning, mid-afternoon, and an hour before bedtime. (We normally did not gain weight in spite of the amount of food we were eating, because of the warm temperature. We would perspire quite a bit, especially during the dry season.) Since we had plenty of food, we always had one or two or three poor relatives staying with us. They, of course, helped with the household chores. We had four or five servants, whom my mother preferred to call "helpers," who got very little pay but free room and board. We had a house boy who cleaned the house and the yard and did other miscellaneous chores. He waxed and polished the hard wood floor once a week, using coconut husks tied to his feet.

In our barrio, like most of the Philippines, we observed the social custom of "*pintakasi.*" *Pintakasi* is sort of a combination work-social thing, where the whole community pitches in to help any family that needs some major project accomplished. We used *pintakasi* to build or repair roofs, fences, anything. A family could have its whole house painted in one weekend. Neighbors, friends, and relatives would come to help. A modest lunch would be served, with the participants helping in its preparation. *Pintakasi* was especially effective if the family had a beautiful daughter, because all the strongest young men would gather and do great work to show off.

In the Philippines, we love to celebrate. We had a barrio fiesta in Don Galo each May and a Paranaque town fiesta each November. We invited friends and relatives from other barrios during our barrio fiesta, and we invited friends and relatives from other towns during our town fiesta. All the barrios and towns staggered the dates of their festivals so that we could all attend as many as we wanted. We celebrated Christmas, New Year's, birthdays, christenings, and weddings. We would even celebrate a person's death, after nine days of praying. Celebrating was so important that people saved money or even borrowed it to hold grand celebrations.

Our family was a happy one, and we had many celebrations of our own. Almost anything gave us an excuse for a party. For instance, we had a celebration when I rescued a small puppy dog. Even everyday life had its party aspects. Every Sunday, we always had a family get-together at home. We went to church early in the morning, and after playing for awhile, we had to be ready for lunch at around twelve. Quite often, we had relatives and family friends join us. It was just simple food of *nilaga* or *sinigang* (boiled meat or chicken or pork, with plenty of vegetables) and fried fish on the side. We ate it with "*patis*" (fish sauce) and sometimes home made "*bago-ong*"(salted tiny shrimps or fish). We ate tons of rice. Sometimes, we would have *cari-cari* or *menudo* or *pinakbit* or *paksiw* or *adobo* or *tinola* or *pansit* or *lumpia*. Those are native foods that my mother, Inang, loved to prepare. She would sometimes cook Spanish dishes, but only on special occasions. Sometimes, but not often, we would have oysters and broiled pork. Everyone, including guests, helped in food preparation and clean up. Quite often, we ended up in the living room singing, with my brother, Kaka Mando, at the piano. ("Kaka" is a term of affection and respect we use for our elders.) It was a poor man's party.

Not just Sundays, but many evenings, our family sang after supper, as Kaka Mando played and sang. Like my mother, he was a good singer. He sang like Bing Crosby, the singer he loved to emulate. My younger sister, Lourdes, was good at the piano, a great singer, and an excellent ballroom dancer. My big sister, Kaka Cely, took piano lessons for over ten years, but she could only play one piece. Her singing was okay, but nothing to brag about. My younger brother, Tommy, and I were poor piano players. Our singing talents left much to be desired. My mother could really sing. She was a great singer. Though our talents varied, we all loved to gather together and raise our voices in song.

Our house was torn down and replaced with a larger one, built of first-class materials, about 1935. On the second floor, we had a huge living room, four bedrooms, a dining room, and a kitchen. The second floor also had a toilet, complete with French bidet, and a separate room with a bathtub and a shower. We had running water with strong water pressure. On the ground floor, we had a small kitchenette and a living/dining area. We had three small rooms, used as bedrooms, down there, another toilet, and a garage. Those old clay cooking pots and the wood-burning stoves I remember so well were replaced with steel or aluminum cookware and an electric stove. With seven bedrooms, running water, an electric stove, and two toilets, we lived quite the luxurious life, by our standards. Our house had always been a center of our barrio's social life, but with the new house—especially the huge living room upstairs, which was perfect for dancing—we became "party central."

We had fruit trees in our back yard and a tall, large, flowering tree called "*ilang ilang*." After the war came and I entered the guerrillas, we often climbed the *ilang ilang* to the roof to hide, when the Japanese were rounding up the locals for the "*zona*." I will tell you about "*zona*" later. For now, just know that the *ilang ilang* saved my life more than once.

When the war broke out, we had a1937 Buick. Before the Buick, we had had an old gasser, a 1924 Stutz. We had an old refrigerator bought in the early thirties. We had a combination radio/phonograph and a piano, bought long before I was born. We did not have a washing machine, so all washing had to be done by hand. We did not have a TV set, even as late as 1951, when I left for America. A telephone was installed around 1936.

There were three wooden houses in our block. Across the street, my father owned another lot, and we had a basketball court built there. On the lot across the twenty-foot-wide road were four small houses and a little 24-hour café. The block to the left of the basketball court had three houses, one of which belonged to Stella's family. Her house, a two-story wooden framed house, was at the corner of the block, so her house and ours were diagonally opposite. While our house was the largest in the neighborhood, Stella's was larger than most others. Her father, a pianist, had died when she was young. However, her mother ran a successful meat business, then married a judge (who, incidentally, became a congressman and, after the war, a senator).

When I was about two years old, there were no children my age around our neighborhood for me to play with, other than my older sister, Kaka Cely, who is two years older. She had friends her age and some even older. Her friends came to play with her in our house, as we had plenty of space to play in. I had to join and play with them, but they did not want me as a playmate—they claimed that I was a pest. They always said that I needed a baby sitter, that I was too young to be with them. My big brother, Kaka Mando, was eight years older than I, already a big boy while I was still a baby, and he also did not want to play or babysit with me. My younger brother Tommy and sister Lourdes were not even born yet.

We had a number of cousins and relatives who were frequently with us, but they were much older and not as pretty as my sister's playmates. Kaka Cely's friends were pretty, and I just loved to be with them. I had been wearing, at the time, mostly hand-me-down clothes from Kaka Mando, which I loved to wear—the *mamilocco* (pants with suspenders), still in style even today. Kaka Mando's pants were too large for me, but I did not mind. That is, I did not mind until the girls started teasing me for wearing those over-sized pants.

I hated the teasing, and I would cry endlessly until Inang would let me wear the same clothes the girls were wearing. Kaka Cely had plenty of outgrown dresses, which fit me well; I loved to wear them, day in and day out. The girls started calling me "*bakla*", meaning gay or girlish. It did not bother me, as I did not understand the meaning of it. Even after the meaning of the word was explained to me, it meant nothing to me. I was, after all, hardly more than an infant.

The girls loved to outsmart me. For instance, whenever we got some kind of fruit, like guavas or *siniguelas* (similar to a small peach) or mangoes, they would say loudly, for me to hear, that they wanted the small, green ones. Of course, I would take up the chorus, saying I wanted the small, green ones, too. I was the loudest of all, and I would always get the hard little fruits. They would end up eating their big, ripe fruits, laughing with joy while I ended up crying. I do not know why this trick continued to work, but it did for quite awhile. Maybe it took awhile for me to realize why they were laughing at me.

I was about three years old when Inang gave me the worst punishment I ever had from her. I have had many of those, but the spanking she gave me this time was so painful that it still sticks in my mind. Kaka Cely had told her that I was a bad boy, for I had been lifting their dresses. I told Inang that I simply wanted to know if they were wearing something underneath, for I had nothing under my dress. I did not understand what was wrong with it.

I still remember a few of those friends of Kaka Cely's, for whom I had some kind of puppy love. One was Anita. She was so beautiful. I loved her the most. She stopped coming to our house, though, and I kept asking, "Why?" When they told me she was sick, I told Kaka Cely and Inang that I wanted to go to her house to see her. They refused, saying I might catch her sickness. "When will she get well and come back?" I would ask.

Always, the answer was, "Soon." She never came back. Years later, when I was about six or maybe seven, I finally understood why. She died of leprosy at a very young age of ten.

I was also in love with Clara and Conception, but they were older than Anita and were not as beautiful. There were two other girls, whose names I cannot remember, who liked me though I did not like them. They were both fat.

The girls would continuously tease me, whether I wore a dress or the over-sized *mamilocco*. Things changed when I went to preschool wearing those *mamiloccos*. I had grown fast, and those suspendered trousers now fit me well. I think they must have been very becoming. I was very happy and proud as my pants were of good quality, colorful, and expensive. My school mates were very envious of me, for I was always well-dressed and always wore good shoes. Most of the boys had no proper shoes. They wore wooden shoes or slippers. The girls did not call me *bakla* anymore. I continued to be very much interested in girls and at age nine, I got caught making out with my first girl friend.

Stella lived across the street from us. She was two years younger than me, too young to be friends with my sister, and therefore too young to be part of my world. I knew who she was, but I scarcely noticed her then.

I went to first grade at the Don Galo Elementary School, at age five. I attended the Don Galo Elementary School from first to fourth grade. My first grade teacher was my godmother, which was why I was admitted at an early age. First graders had to be six years old, and some were even seven. I was the smallest first grader, but thanks to my father, when it came to arithmetic, I was even better than the second graders and some third graders. That made my father very proud.

My mother walked me to my first day of school. She continued to do that until I had met some schoolmates to walk with. I believed I was already a big boy who needed no escort, though, so sometimes I would walk by myself if the other kids were late getting to my house to pick me up.

When I went to Don Galo Elementary School, I "brown bagged" for lunch. My mother would sometimes ask me to tell my friends not to bring lunch for the following day. Then, with the help of a relative staying with us, she would bring a delicious hot lunch—the catch of the day from my father's fish pond, native deserts, and sodas, enough for five or six of us. There were some kids, not my friends, who had no lunch food; my mother would ask them to join us. I loved the whole thing, which we did so many times.

I made many friends at school. They were mostly older than I was. Most of them lived in the north end of Don Galo where the school was located. We lived in the south end.

We played in the rain after school and on weekends during the almost six months of rainy days. The rain water was mostly warm; even when, occasionally, it was cold, that did not matter, with all the running and horsing around we were doing.

Kaka Mando taught me how to swim in the river. There was no swimming pool in the whole town of Paranaque. I went swimming with my school friends during summer, and by the age of seven I was able to swim across the 150-foot-wide river and back. We jumped, feet first, off the 25-foot-high bridge into the water—and eventually we learned to dive in head first. The salty water took care of any cuts, wounds, or skin disease we might have. We always came out of the summer vacation very healthy and very well tanned

I learned to ride a bike, using Kaka Mando's bike, when I was eight. My friends and I began taking boats to distant fields for picnics. We brought canned sardines and rolls, and we would pick fruits, like mangoes and guavas, from the fields. We never asked permission to pick fruit—which is to say, we stole it. Honestly, that was fun. We did that many times. My older friends often had cigarettes. That was when I started learning to smoke.

I also started playing mahjong when I was about nine. My friends and I became enthusiastic about basketball. We already were interested in girls. I liked cars, too, an interest I could indulge because of our family's relative wealth. One thing that set me apart from my new friends was an interest in the piano. When I started learning to play, my friends would say that piano is for girls only. None of my friends had a piano at home. This interest in the piano, and its distinction from my friends' interests, will be important to our story later on.

By the time I was about ten, the pattern my life would follow, until the war, had begun to take shape. I became inseparable from my closest friends in Don Galo, mostly boys two to four years older than I, mostly poor kids. We smoked—American cigarettes, "Piedmont," because they were cheapest—and gambled and spent immense amounts of time at sports. We played basketball most of the time and had some success. We were really not any better than most other teams, but we were tougher. We were bullies, really. We would beat up other boys from the next barrio whenever they would show any interest with the girls of Don Galo.

Eight of us became a steady group, and we stayed together for years. A lot of people did not like us. My parents got complaints from many parents that we were behaving like "gangsters." That word did not really describe us fairly, though we affected the styles of gangsters—we wore long hair and did not shave regularly, for instance. I had seen a movie in which Latin gangsters wore high-waisted pants, so we wore that style, to my parents' consternation.

We were rough, I suppose, and we ruled the barrio, at least among the kids. But none of us had ever owned guns or knives. We were not involved in drugs or real crime. We smoked cigarettes, but no pot. We did not even drink alcohol. There was a lot of gambling. Weekends and during school vacation, we made money playing mahjong. We were very good at it. We were not exactly cheating but were just good at it. When it came to mahjong, I was the brain. As we grew older, we added other forms of gambling to our activities—poker, craps, and *sabong*, which is cockfighting

I was not the gang leader. Our gang leader, Hiling Pascual, was two years older than I. He was really a tough guy. Pareng Hiling did not stand for insults or deception, and his loyalty to his friends had no bounds. ("Pareng" is a term of affection used for one's close friends.) He was strong and quick, and he stood up for his dignity vigorously. More than once, he put people in the hospital, for he would beat them severely when they did something wrong to him or his friends. Fearless and proud, he really gave our gang its fearsome reputation.

He was not one of those people who picks fights, though—he only fought for what he thought was right—and he had a good sense of humor. We called him "Tambok." The top of his left foot was enlarged, or *tambok* in Tagalog. He was ashamed of it, so as boys will do, we made it his nickname. It was really nothing and could have been easily removed surgically, but he did not want that done. Later in life, I was the godfather of his first daughter and therefore his *compadre*—a spiritual brother.

Evenings, we spent hours and hours on the beach, watching the almost-nightly "show," smoking while waiting for the main event. What "show"? Because the Philippines is so beautiful, and because everything there was very cheap by foreign standards, some foreigners moved there and lived like kings, though they had just ordinary wealth in their own countries. A dozen or so had homes in Don Galo, along the beach facing Manila bay. The fashion was to build the houses with their shower rooms facing the sunset, with glass walls from floor to ceiling. In about half a dozen of the homes, the nightly show was excellent. The "stars of the show" were beautiful—and very clean, taking nightly showers. While they performed to an appreciative, if unacknowledged, audience, we did what normal adolescent boys would be doing at such an entertainment.

Though I had become something of a ruffian, and though my parents were not happy with me, they were very lenient. With Kaka Mando, they had tried being strict, and it had not worked. With me, though they voiced their displeasure very clearly, they tried the tactic of letting me find my own way. They were still very kind and loving.

I went to school in Manila from grade five and on. I therefore had friends from Manila, and elsewhere, who were not members of our gang. I began to develop something of a double life—my tough-guy life in Don Galo and a different one in Manila.

In the elementary grades from five to seven, I attended (and graduated with honors from) the Philippine Normal School in Manila, where the teachers were mostly Americans. After the Philippines became a U.S. possession, the Americans reversed the long-time policy of the Spaniards. The Americans believed in public education for all. They sent ten thousand teachers to educate Filipino children. The first group of teachers came on the boat "U.S.S. Thomas," and we called all the teachers "Thomasites." I was very fortunate to have had the privilege of receiving an education under American teachers, for they worked in the Philippines a relatively short time. When the Philippines became a commonwealth country in 1935, the U.S. teachers were mostly replaced by local ones. I was among the last group of Filipino students to study under the Americans.

We had a driver to take us—Kaka Cely and me—to school each day. I would get up early in the morning and drive our car around Don Galo. The driver then would dust or wash the car before heading for the school in Manila. It was always dusty in Don Galo except when it was raining.

Usually the driver picked us up after school. Sometimes, though, Amang and Inang would surprise us. They would meet us after school for a family outing to the zoo or a movie, followed by dinner in a nice restaurant.

I said that my life in Manila became different from my life in Don Galo. I must tell you how this came about. At first, I was as rough and ill-mannered in Manila as on the streets of Don Galo. When I was in the sixth grade, though, there was an incident, when I was suspended for the third time, that changed my school behavior radically, forever.

After this third suspension, the school principal sent me home with instructions to bring my parents to meet with her. I could not bring myself to tell my father that I was suspended again, so I asked Kaka Mando, who was just over twenty-one years old at that time, to come in their stead. I lied to Kaka Mando, telling him that I was sent home for being too noisy in the classroom. In truth, Mrs. Richardson, my sixth-grade teacher, had reported me to the principal for making out with my girlfriend in school.

We went to see the school principal, a Filipina woman named Mrs. Ruperto, who had just taken over the job from an American lady. She was trying to do a good job, to live up to the new standards of American education. The principal was not too happy that I brought my older brother instead of my father. At first, she did not even think that he was my older brother. I was taller than him, and I had a very dark complexion, while he was very light, like our mother. Perhaps worse, although he was well dressed, his face was swollen and battered—he had just won the Philippines amateur college boxing championship (in the bantamweight division) the day before. She thought he was some ruffian I had picked up on the street to pretend to be my elder brother. He was able to convince her that we were brothers, from similarities in our facial structures and the sounds of our voices, and from the name on his driver's license.

Mrs. Ruperto started lecturing me and reading from her notebook: (1) Suspended three months earlier for fighting with a girl during recess inside the class room. (2) Suspended last month for gambling with two other boys during lunch break (3) Suspended four days earlier for kissing a girl in the hallway during class hours.

Upon hearing the real reason I was suspended for the third time, Kaka Mando looked at me with big, angry eyes, like he wanted to kill me. Mrs. Ruperto, a very smart lady, realized that I had not told him the real reason why I was suspended. She was furious and adamantly insisted that I get my father or mother to her office.

Kaka Mando, no matter how angry he was, did not want to make the situation worse, so he told her that our parents were in Zamboanga, on the island of Mindinao, and wouldn't be back till the following month. That was not true, but we had agreed upon that excuse in advance. (That was very smart planning, for Mrs. Ruperto asked me separately why my parents were not there, and I gave her the same story.) She decided to accept my brother as my responsible substitute parent, if he agreed to punish me in her presence. He agreed.

At her instruction, I was laid on the library table on my stomach. Mrs. Ruperto gave Kaka Mando a solid, round bamboo stick about three-quarters of an inch in diameter. Kaka Mando whipped me, very hard, on my behind. After about seven or eight lashes, Mrs. Ruperto stopped him. I felt great relief; I thought that it had not been too bad, even though it had hurt a lot.

My relief was premature; she just wanted to show him how to do it right. She hit me three times. Kaka Mando was a quick learner, and he resumed his task in earnest. After a million lashes, it seemed, she motioned that I had had enough.

My butt was kind of numb. I was crying, not only because I was hurting, but from betrayal. My girl friend, Monserrat, had lied when Mrs. Richardson saw us kissing, claiming that I was doing it without her permission. I did not blame Kaka Mando for doing what he had to do, but I was heartbroken that Monserrat's lie had put me in such a terrible situation.

Before we left, Mrs. Blue, the school superintendent, joined the meeting. Her parting words to us were that my next suspension would be an expulsion. That was quite a lesson.

Of course, Kaka Mando was so angry that he told everyone about the incident, and they never let me forget it. I could never, ever have forgotten that whipping incident, anyway.

My school behavior after that was hard to believe. I finished that grade, and the seventh grade, too, with honors. From that point on, my behavior in school changed—though in Don Galo, I remained the "gangster."

Though I had still not taken notice of Stella, apparently she had noticed me. She hated me so much that she would not talk to me; she branded me as a "bandido" or gangster, and called my group "Rudy's gang." I did not know any of that until later.

Stella had taken piano lessons from an early age, and she spent plenty of time practicing piano, which I could not help but hear. Sometime around age of fourteen or so, I began enjoying the sorts of music she played—classical pieces, I now know. I would often listen to her play, though she did not know this. I still had no personal interest in her, though. She was just the skinny girl across the road who played lovely music.

Stella and I went to different schools, and we had different groups of friends. We had very little opportunity to see each other. If I saw her, alone or with friends or other people, I would, of course, smile, wave, and say, "Hello." Everyone would reciprocate except her. She hardly acknowledged my friendly gestures. That did not bother me, then. She was never really on my mind. In time, that would change.

Chapter Two

History of a Pro-American

As you can see, my family and I had a very good life. However, the political situation in the Philippines was very complicated and difficult.

If I claimed that I was some kind of deep political thinker back in those days, you probably wouldn't believe me. After all, I've already told you the things that occupied my attention—sports, gambling, girls, and cars, not necessarily in that order. But we had been an occupied land since the sixteenth century. First the Spaniards, then the Americans, colonized our islands. In an occupied country, the occupation occupies your mind.

History is not a just boring school subject when you live under the control of another nation. It is the flavor of your life. Colonialism and hopes for freedom are part of everyday life, as much as the central market or the sunset. You think about these things, and they shape who you are. When I was a boy, the worst of colonialism was not long past, and hopes for freedom were high.

Remember, I had been hearing about these things since those long walks with my father when I was just a small boy. My father had been active against the Spaniards. I knew about the history of our country's subjugation the same way an American kid around the year 1800 would have known about America's history with England and its Revolutionary War. I knew our history like I knew the road to Manila.

You cannot understand Filipino reaction to World War II, or my decisions in those days, unless you know something about this. If you will just stay with me for a few pages, you will see what I am getting at. If you hate history, you can skip to the next chapter.

A few Filipinos prospered obscenely under the colonialists, but most did not. Most Filipinos suffered very badly in every way. Remember that my family had lived through liberation from Spain, the first attempts at freedom, and America's crushing of those attempts. By the time I was a boy, though, the Americans had done many good things for the Philippines. We were even on the way to becoming a free country under American tutelage. My father was strongly pro-American, and he made sure everyone in our family understood how much America had done for our country.

Our family was so fanatically pro-American that when Kaka Mando's son was born in late1944, he refused to have him christened immediately, insisting that the boy's godfather would be the first American soldier that the boy saw when General MacArthur returned to free us from Japan. Kaka Mando held firm to that resolve, and an American soldier, Edward Wadarsky, did indeed become the boy's godfather. Mr. Wadarsky will play a significant role in this story before we are done.

When Ferdinand Magellan "discovered" our islands in March of 1521, we were not a nation. About 1,000 of our 7,000 islands were populated by many different tribes and local social structures. Some of the inhabitants were native tribes, like the Ilongot and the Ifugaos, but most of the people were of Malay origin. The Malay had come to the islands over a thousand years earlier. The Chinese, Indonesian, Japanese, and Indian had been trading with the islands' people for over five hundred years, and people from each of these places had settled in our islands.

The lack of any central religious, political, or social organization made it easy for the Spaniards to colonize the islands. There was no organized power to oppose them. The name, "The Philippines," comes from the name of King Philip II, the Spanish monarch under whom colonization took place in earnest.

Spain got serious about taking over our islands in 1565, when King Philip ordered his officials in Mexico—then part of the Spanish Empire—to send an expedition to establish control. Miguel Legazpi headed the expedition. The Spanish wanted to use the Philippines as a stepping stone for trade with other Asian countries—ships could go from Mexico to the Philippines and use it as a trading post. They also wanted to boost the influence and prestige of the Spanish Empire by making the Philippines an outpost of Spanish society.

The Spanish exploited the natives mercilessly. They "drafted" thousands of natives to work on projects profiting the Spaniards, like cutting timber, building ships, and working the fields. These draftees were basically slaves. The Spaniards looted native homes, stealing any treasures they wanted. They imposed heavy taxes. They enforced their economic rule with violence—which often carried over to rampant rape and murder.

These abuses caused unrest and protest. The uprisings and revolts never lasted long, though—they were strictly local, and the natives lacked the resources and organization for strong resistance. The Spaniards were brutal in suppressing them, however, establishing a history of vicious, violent oppression, which bred resentful submission.

The Spanish Government gave huge land grants to Spaniards who would come to the Philippines to settle. They would also allow Spanish soldiers to seize tracts of land for themselves. The Spanish gave these landed elite the feudal powers of medieval lords. To this day, the descendants of these petty tyrants control the economy of the Philippines. By the time I was a boy, of course, this elite consisted mostly of mixed-blood Filipino descendants of the Spanish lords. By now, they were Filipino, but their interests and loyalties were very different from most Filipinos'—including my family's and mine.

The Spaniards also gave the Philippines Catholicism. The priests were concerned with more than heavenly matters. I have already mentioned this, in explaining how my mother's distinguished family became impoverished.

You must understand that the priests had far greater control over the Philippines than the politicians had. The Philippines was administered a Governor General, who reported to the Viceroy of Mexico, who reported to the King of Spain in Madrid. Spanish governors were thus "low men on the totem pole" of Spanish rulers. Madrid focused attention on the Philippines only from time to time—sometimes, the position of Governor General would be vacant for years. As a minor post, it was often used as a sop in Spanish politics, with first one then another Spanish faction getting this little plum. There was great turnover in the Governor Generalship.

Not so with the power structure of the church in the Philippines. The priests basically ruled themselves, and they had great longevity and stability. The priests had time and manpower to consolidate their position, often with no Governor General in place to oppose them, never with one who had been in power so long as they had. Not only that—the church had vast land holdings itself. It was itself a medieval kingdom.

The priests not only got control of people's spiritual lives, but they had economic power and domination of the secular government. You have to realize that these priests were Spaniards. Spanish priests rigidly discouraged Filipinos from becoming priests, and when they did allow them to enter the priesthood, they kept the Filipino priests subordinate in the church hierarchy. This would be one of the things that eventually caused the people to rise up in revolt.

Between the brutality of Spanish officials, the economic power of the landed elite, and the iron fist of the friars, most Filipinos were pretty well beaten into submission. However, in 1762, the British sailed into Manila Bay and defeated the Spanish. Though the Brits only stayed a couple of years before leaving on their own, the easy way they beat the Spaniards showed the Filipinos that the oppressors were not invincible. That is really when the revolutionary movement got started. Ideas of revolt, as well as many uprisings, became more widespread. Over the next hundred years, revolutionaries built a substantial following.

By about 1870, the Spaniards had trouble on their hands. By now, the landed elite consisted of mixed-blood Filipinos who resented Spanish domination. The Filipino clergy were tired of submitting to the Spanish clergy. Neither of those groups could be called democratic; they just wanted power handed over to them. But they were important in motivating people to oppose Spain. Poverty was worse than ever—during the nineteenth century, the Spaniards had converted a lot of land from growing food to growing sugar and tobacco for export, so people did not even have enough to eat. Ordinary people were crying for relief and reform.

The first effective revolt happened in Cavite, a Spanish arsenal just south of Paranaque, in 1872. Instigated by educated Filipinos and some wealthy landed elite, three hundred soldiers mutinied and murdered their Spanish officers. It was, unfortunately, quickly suppressed. The government, controlled by Spanish priests, used it as an excuse to liquidate three leading Filipino priests, Fathers Burgos, Gomez, and Zamora, who had campaigned for the rights of Filipino clergy. Their garroting awakened powerful popular sentiments for reform and revolution. The priests became legends.

Our first really great popular hero, Jose Rizal, wrote that the death of the priests stirred him to the side of reform. He was from one of the elite families, educated and living in Europe. With Marcelo del Pilar, Graciano Jaena, and the Luna brothers, he formed a Propaganda Movement to build support for reform. The Propagandists, as they called themselves, published a reformist magazine in Spain called *La Solidaridad* ("Solidarity") from 1889 to 1895. Dr. Rizal was a genius. He was an eye surgeon, linguist, painter, sculptor, novelist, poet, dramatist, scientist, and historian. The Cavite mutiny in 1872 inspired him to write two great novels: *Noli Me Tangere* (*Touch Me Not*) in 1887 and *El Filibusterismo* (*The Subversive*) in 1891. The books portrayed authoritarianism and abuses by the friars and the government. The Spanish government in the Philippines banned those books, but they were widely available "underground." They really focused people's attention and stirred the passions of reform.

Upon his return to the Philippines in 1892, Dr. Rizal founded "La Liga Filipina" ("The Philippine League"), an organization aimed at peaceful reform. Dr. Rizal's fate illustrates the stupidity and rigid anti-Filipino stance of the government. Dr. Rizal was not a revolutionary. He believed that power should remain with the elite, but that the Philippines should be assimilated into Spain as a self-governing province, and that Filipinos should have the same rights as the Spaniards. What he was opposed to, was unfair treatment of the people. He was exiled to Dapitan in Mindanao, accused falsely of being a revolutionary agitator.

Dr. Rizal could have escaped the Philippines during his four years of exile in Dapitan, but he chose not to and was arrested. His trial for rebellion, sedition, and illicit association was a mere formality; the rulers just wanted to get rid of him. My father took part in protests in support of Dr. Rizal. On December 30, 1896, Rizal was executed by firing squad, at a very young age of 35, in what is now named Rizal Park in Manila. It was a major blunder by the Spaniards, for it made the people even angrier and intensified the demand for change—but now, by way of revolution, not peaceful reform.

The next important leader of the brewing revolution, our second great hero, was Andres Bonifacio, a man born and raised in poverty. He founded the *Katipunan*, the full name of which meant, "The Highest and Most Respectable Association of the Sons of the People," shortly after Dr. Rizal was deported to Dapitan. The objective of the secret association, very different from Dr. Rizal's, was independence by way of revolution.

The membership grew rapidly, and in 1896, the Spaniards, goaded by the friars, started making thousands of arbitrary arrests, with hundreds of executions. At Balintawak, north of Manila, Bonifacio tore up his *cedula* (tax certificate) and called for independence, urging his followers to rise in arms. That was the famous "Cry of Balintawak," which signaled the start of the revolution. Bonifacio and Emilio Jacinto, with hundreds of followers, led an attack on the Spanish garrison at San Juan del Monte in Metro Manila. Simultaneously, eight provinces around Manila revolted. The revolution spread to other islands.

Bonifacio failed in many battles and lost popularity among his followers. One of his young soldiers, Emilio Aguinaldo, won several battles in his native Cavite province and emerged as the revolutionary leader. Aguinaldo, like Rizal a son of the wealthy landed elite, had joined Bonafacio once Rizal's movement had been destroyed. With Aguinaldo's rise to power, the revolution shifted its aims to those helpful to the elite.

Now the situation was really complicated. Bonifacio's Katipunan organization was replaced by the new "revolutionary government" with Aguinaldo as the President. The revolutionaries themselves tried and executed Bonifacio for sedition. The popular legend was that Aguinaldo wanted him to be exiled but was overruled by his advisors. The advisors argued that Bonifacio was a threat to the landed elite, who were important in opposing the Spaniards.

The government, frustrated by its inability to crush the rebellion, arranged a peace agreement with Aguinaldo, known as "The Pact of Biak-na Bato." The pact gave peace but without reforms. This did not sit well with many of the revolutionaries. Aguinaldo was an important historical figure, but when I was growing up, he was not regarded as a hero, like Dr. Rizal and Bonifacio.

At the very same time, Commodore George Dewey of the U.S. Navy had been sent to the Philippines to attack the Spanish navy as part of The Spanish-American War. The result was "The Battle of Manila Bay," one of the most one-sided battles in naval history as Dewey destroyed the

Spanish armada. The Spanish Governor needed help and asked Aguinaldo for his support to fight the Americans, with all kinds of reform promises. Aguinaldo, on the other hand, was assured by the Americans that they came as liberators, with promises that the Philippines would be just like America, a free democratic country. Aguinaldo refused the government's overtures and threw his support to the Americans. His volunteer army routed the Spanish forces on land, just as Admiral Dewey had done by sea. President Emilio Aguinaldo declared Philippine independence on June 12, 1898, ending over three centuries of Spanish rule.

The Americans took no notice of this proclamation of independence. They still considered the Philippines a Spanish possession, something to be bargained over at the end of the Spanish-American War. The Treaty of Paris, which ended that war, ceded the Philippines, Guam and Puerto Rico to the United States of America, while selling the Philippines to the U.S. for $20 million. The American colonization of the Philippines officially began on December 10, 1898. The Filipinos defied American sovereignty, proclaiming the First Philippine Republic on January 23, 1899. General Emilio Aguinaldo was proclaimed president.

The Philippine-American war, also known as the War of Philippine Independence, started on February 4, 1899, after an American shot a Filipino soldier in an old section of what is now Metro Manila. Aguinaldo immediately declared war against the United States. The new colony was quickly subdued, as the Americans had superior arms and well-trained forces. It did not help that many Filipinos had lost faith in Aguinaldo, since he had revealed that he had no passion to demand reform that would help the common people. He was a good soldier, but not a good leader of the people.

General Arthur MacArthur, father of Douglas MacArthur, in charge of the American operation, drove Aguinaldo and his forces to northern Luzon. Aguinaldo disbanded his army, with orders to institute guerrilla warfare, and hid in Palanan, in the province of Isabela. He was captured in June of 1901, which marked the fall of the First Philippines Republic and the end of effective resistance. Aguinaldo asked the Filipinos to accept the American sovereignty. (When I returned to the Philippines in the late 1950s, I got to know him pretty well, for in his retirement he was my neighbor in Don Galo.)

President Theodore Roosevelt then declared that the Philippines had been "pacified." It had taken over 70,000 U.S. troops, who killed over 200,000 Filipinos, to subdue the new colony. Sporadic insurgency continued for many more years, particularly in the island of Mindanao.

The Americans were well accepted all over most of the Philippines, especially in Manila and the provinces around. The story was somewhat different in the southern part of Mindanao, which was largely Muslim. The Americans considered the Muslims or *Moros* as barbarians, savages, a wild and ignorant people. The Americans waged an ugly war against the *Moros*, marked by racism and atrocities. Entire towns were burned to the ground. In one village, every male over ten years old was shot.

It may seem strange that the Americans were so well accepted in most of the country after putting down The First Philippine Republic so violently. However, if you keep in mind the situation in our country, it becomes easy to understand.

To start with, President Aguinaldo had failed to enlist the fervent passions of the common people, since his true loyalty lay with the landed elite. The Americans bought off Aguinaldo's supporters by letting the landed elite keep their lands and economic privileges. They even did more than that—they stripped the Catholic church of its vast landholdings and gave most of them to the landed elite.

The American colonial government freed ordinary people from the power of the church and bondage to the Spanish government. They brought in education and democracy. I have already mentioned "The Thomasites," the American teachers who came to the Philippines. Both through the education system and through direct action, the Americans taught principles of democracy and uprooted many of the corrupt local officials. By 1907, the Philippines was holding elections for offices and even had a kind of elected national legislature. You remember that my father was an elected official, a town councilman. He was a very moral man. Because of the Americans, many people like my father, who really cared about helping the people, had replaced the corrupt, self-seeking officials of the Spanish rule. The Americans also developed a public health system, improved the roads, and built a better communications system.

Back then, I mostly knew that the Americans had improved our basic living conditions greatly. I did not yet understand that they had not changed some basic problems and had even introduced new ones. Their policies favored the landed elite, which allowed the feudal structure to endure, and favored the American businessmen even more. The Philippines was flooded with American goods, while native resources were taken for use by American corporations. Still, the freedom from overt oppression meant that we had more rights and less corruption—and more people had enough to eat. As imperialists go, the Americans were a big improvement on the Spaniards.

Most important, in 1935, America gave us the status of a commonwealth, with some powers of self-government, and promised us complete independence in ten years. Manuel Quezon was inaugurated as president of the commonwealth. This was a great thing for us. We now thought of ourselves as a nation moving toward freedom. Quezon introduced a social justice program to quell unrest among the poverty-stricken masses, while simultaneously protecting the basic powers of the landed elites. He did not challenge the basic economic structure; he tried to end the worst abuses and keep common people happy enough to avoid revolution.

I don't claim that I cared a lot about politics back then. I was an ordinary kid, who happened to know a lot of history because he had a father who cared about such things. But the way I saw it back then, when the war arrived, we were on the way to freedom for the first time in our history. The Japanese wanted to make us their colony—and when the Japanese took over a country, they were worse than the Spaniards had ever been. Some Filipinos doubted that the U.S. would bother to come back and free the Philippines. In our family, that was not even a consideration. Some Filipinos thought they should accept and accommodate the new rulers. For my family, that was beyond the pale. We were pro-American, pro-democracy, and pro-independence.

Chapter Three

Boy Guerrilla in Love

On Monday, December 8, 1941, (which was Sunday, December 7, in the U.S.), I went to school, as usual. I was seventeen years old, in the third year of high school. All the students were sent home—Pearl Harbor had been bombed.

I was actually very happy, because my girl friend of the moment and I had been ditching classes for many weeks. The school had written my parents about it, but at least on this day we could spend our time having fun instead of going to school, without any bad consequences.

Though Don Galo was only four miles from Nichols Air Base, a U.S. military installation, I wasn't concerned about the war. We were told at school that Hawaii was over five thousand miles away from the Philippines, so I told my girl friend that there was nothing to worry about. Pearl Harbor was so far away, and the United States would beat the Hell out of the Japs. We went off and had a nice day.

Around four o'clock the next morning, I was at home, in bed, asleep, when the loudest noise I've ever heard woke me up. A bomb had rattled our very-solid house; I thought we had taken a direct hit. Everyone in the family ran to my parents' bedroom. We were all frightened—most of us were crying. More bombs went off—we realized Nichols was under attack.

Even my father did not know what to do. He was honestly scared, completely unprepared to face this dangerous situation. He phoned a lawyer-friend in Manila; the friend, who was also surprised by the Jap attack, just told my father to move out of Don Galo.

We did not yet have an air-raid shelter at home, so my father told us to go downstairs, to the ground floor, directly under the bathroom/toilet area. That part of the house rested on an eight-inch thick, reinforced concrete slab, so it was the strongest and the safest part of the house.

All day long, Japanese planes kept dropping big bombs on Nichols Field. Every bomb sounded so loud, as if our house or the house next door were being hit. Terror and confusion filled our minds—we had never had such an experience before, and we certainly never expected it.

We were also very hungry. Children throughout the neighborhood wept from hunger, fear, and confusion. Amang went to his bakery to get some day-old rolls—the bakery, of course, did not bake that day. Later, a cousin who was staying with us slaughtered a couple of chickens and, after a fashion, cooked them with a huge pot of rice. However, the power lines had been destroyed, and we only had an electric stove; we had to gather some wood and improvise a wood stove. While the bombs were dropping, we ate a crude combination of raw and burned rice, undercooked and burned chicken. We all ate voraciously, though, except my mother. Terror still filled our minds, but our full bellies quieted our weeping.

We stayed under the concrete slab during days of continuous bombing. The first day was unbearable; by the second, we had kind of had gotten used to it, except for Kaka Mando's children. Lilia was six years old,

Marietta was five, Corazon was four, and Charito was three. They cried endlessly, which drove everyone crazy. We all slept, as well as we could, crowded into the tiny space, some on the floor and some on cots.

In our helplessness, fear, and fatigue, we argued a lot, about things both trivial and crucial. The kids kept on saying that they did not like Don Galo, that there were so many bombs in Don Galo—as if we could do anything about that. Kaka Mando wanted to take our family away from Don Galo, to a house in Obando, Bulacan, that my father owned. That was a small house, which would hold no more than a few of us. Kaka Mando insisted he would take his family only, but Inang would not let that happen. She loved her grandchildren so much—she would not let them be separated from her. That created more arguments, crying, and shouting, while the bombs were falling and the Japs wouldn't quit.

On the evening of the third day, my father's tenants in his Balintawak house—six miles north of Manila—called to say they were leaving my father's house to go back to their home province. That solved one problem—the Balintawak house was big enough for all of us—but the bomb problem would not go away. We were not sure traveling would be safe.

On the fourth day, though, during a lull in the bombing, we packed our Buick and drove north to Balintawak. Once the family was safe, I had to drive back to Don Galo to get all the cooking, sleeping, and personal goods I could. I filled the car to the ceiling. While I was on my way back to Balintawak, a few squadrons of Japanese bombers carpet-bombed Nichols Field just a few minutes before I reached the town nearest it, Baclaran. In the main street of Baclaran, panicked people ran wildly in all directions. I saw a man who was hurt, being helped by some people, and I stopped to lend assistance—but before I even reached him, he died. People begged me to take them away, anywhere, wherever I was going. I took an elderly couple—the wife had a small, bleeding wound—and one other person. That was all I could squeeze into the already-packed car. Some people wanted to ride on the hood, but I could not allow that—it would be just too dangerous for everyone.

Within a couple of weeks, just before Christmas, 1941, the U.S. took over our house in Don Galo as storage and officers quarters.

The news was that the U.S. was losing badly. That was evident, as Japanese planes were all over the skies without any U.S. planes in sight. We were all unhappy—scared and worried to be under the Japanese rule, since we had heard (by radio and newspaper) that the Japanese soldiers were raping women and wantonly killing civilians in countries they occupied in the Far East, and bewildered that a powerful country like the U.S. could be beaten by small country like Japan. We did not know what to expect, but we had no reason to expect anything good, or even any reason to think the U.S. could retake our country.

By the last week in January, 1942, the U.S. had abandoned Paranaque, as MacArthur began withdrawing to Bataan. We moved back to our house in Don Galo. Most families, including Stella's, had fled. We intended to stay put in our home, if possible. In Don Galo, there were no military targets. Only Japanese planes were above, still bombing Nichols air base, and there was still some fighting in Manila, eight miles away. Air raid sirens and blackouts continued, but we knew Don Galo was not in immediate danger.

Or so we thought. About the second week in February, 1942, my parents woke me up to tell me that the Japanese soldiers were deployed on the Paranaque Bridge. Our house was two blocks from the bridge, and my father's bakery was at the foot of the bridge. I told my parents that I would go to the bakery to get some bread. I wasn't being heroic—I was a kid, curious to see what Japanese soldiers looked like.

As I approached the bridge, I could see the soldiers deployed, facing Manila, lying down next to their big machine guns. One of the soldiers saw me and shouted to come towards them. He started telling me something, but I had no idea what. He got mad that I wasn't doing what he said—as if I were ignoring him on purpose. He yelled louder. The longer I did not understand, the madder he got. He started pushing and shoving me and making gestures, and I finally understood that he wanted me to sweep the bridge. I was scared and angry because of the shoving, and I was frustrated because there was no broom in sight. I was scared, not knowing what to do. It dawned on me to use a tree branch with leaves, so I grabbed one and started sweeping. Then the soldier began yelling and pushing again—I figured out that he did not want me in front of the guns. That was fine with me, because I was scared to death, sweeping in front of those big guns. When I finished sweeping, I was on the wrong end of the bridge. I was scared to try to walk back across it. Instead, I walked to the barrio of La Huerta, crossed the river by boat to Ibayo, and crossed the bridge from Ibayo to Don Galo. I had left early in the morning and did not come back until lunch time—with no bread. That was the first of my many experiences with the Japanese soldiers and a taste of things to come. If the Japanese intended to "win over" the native population, their soldiers knew exactly how to do the wrong thing.

This was a very hard time for us. We were broken-hearted that the Americans had been defeated so easily. Some people believed the Americans would turn around and expel the Japanese. Others believed they had to reach some accommodation with the new rulers. Life as we knew it had been torn apart, but we did not know what was next.

We listened to short-wave radio news from California, which said that Fil-American forces in Bataan and Corregidor were being badly hammered by the Japanese planes. We didn't need the radio to know that. Pareng Hiling and I had been watching, from the Don Galo beach, the Japanese planes' sustained bombing of Corregidor Island and the Bataan peninsula. Corregidor was in full view, directly in front of Don Galo, while Bataan was a little behind the mountains and to the right of Corregidor. We watched almost every day, hoping that U.S. planes would come out and fight the invaders. They never did. My heart broke as I watched the Japs pulverize the American and Filipino troops relentlessly, without opposition.

The 130,000 Fil-American soldiers in Bataan were defeated by 40,000 Japanese. At the time, we were in despair over what MacArthur had done. My family and friends all agreed that retreating to Bataan was the worst decision MacArthur had made. The geography of Bataan insured that the troops would be trapped, with no food, no supplies, and no escape route. In Bataan, there were wild animals, plenty of venomous snakes, and mosquitos carrying malaria. The jungle was, in many places, virtually impenetrable, and some of the native grasses were as sharp as swords. We could not understand why he had not headed for northern Luzon province—any place there seemed a thousand times better that Bataan. MacArthur's aim was to delay the takeover of the Philippines, and today his retreat gets praise as a masterful operation, but it did not seem smart, to us. He had sacrificed a great number of young lives.

Manila was declared an Open City on February 12, 1942. That "open city" term created new confusion and fear, initially. We did not know at the time what it actually meant. We did not know whether to stay or to go or what dangers we would encounter, where.

The Japanese did everything they could to confiscate all guns and ammunition from Filipino civilians. My father surrendered his shotgun and his .22 caliber semiautomatic Berretta handgun.

Some Filipinos began organizing underground resistance movements immediately, some being coordinated with General MacArthur's forces as early as January, 1942. MacArthur knew he would need prime intelligence and a network of internal fighters already "on the ground" to retake the Philippines, and his people made sure to set up an extensive communications network with the underground before leaving. Most Americans do not realize that Filipino resistance was as strong and vital as the more-celebrated European underground operations. Military documents declassified since the war say we "compared most favorably" with the European guerrillas. (General Charles Willoughby, *The Guerrilla Resistance Movement in The Philippines: 1941-45.*)

Frankly, I had no big need to become a guerrilla, at first. I did not see myself as any kind of hero. But stories began coming in of the atrocities the Japanese soldiers were committing—raping women, torturing and killing people at will. The Japanese seemed to get some kind of big kick out of beheading people by means of swords.

I don't know whether, in itself, that would have made me join the guerrillas. With those stories in my mind, though, and my memories of having to clean the bridge, something else happened.

There were five or six Japanese guard posts between Don Galo and Manila. All Filipino civilians were required to bow to the guards whenever we passed a guard post. No matter what we were doing, where we going, or what bundles we carried, we had to stop, face the guards squarely, and do a ninety-degree bow. The guards were seated; they never bowed back or gave any other acknowledgment.

During the first week of the Japanese occupation, I wanted to go to Manila to get a pair of basketball shoes I had ordered earlier. You must remember that I was still a kid, with an adolescent's concerns. On my way back to Don Galo, as lunchtime approached, I was very hungry and eager to get home. I became sloppy in my bows. At one guard post, I gave the guards a quick fifteen-degree bow, without stopping or squaring off, and continued walking. That was a big mistake.

One of the guards began screaming at me. I did not understand what he was saying, but I knew why he was angry.

He made me stand at attention and turn my face to the noon sun up above. It was a hot day. After a few minutes, my neck got tired, and I let my head slip back into a natural position. The guard screamed and forced my head up again. When I let my head dip forward again, he forced it straight up—and started ripping my mustache hairs out in bunches. He continued this for about half an hour.

When he let me go, my face was sunburned and my upper lip badly torn and swollen. My new shoes were gone—the Japs confiscated them. I was humiliated and outraged. No, it was not nearly as bad as rape or murder; but it was authoritarian, senseless, sadistic, and vicious. Suddenly, the Japanese traits that made their atrocities possible had stared me in the face. I knew that we could not abide the Japanese.

I started asking around about guerrilla organizing. I learned that Juanito Ferrer was organizing a group to fight the Japanese. I was no stranger to the Ferrers. The Ferrers were not only our distant cousins, but were also socially close to my family. I went to Juanito's house in San Dionisio, the barrio neighboring Don Galo, to join the group. Nobody was home except Simeon, Juanito's young brother, who had been a classmate of mine in elementary school. (Years later, Simeon would become a Supreme Court Justice and an enemy of Marcos for declaring Marcos's anti-subversion laws unconstitutional.) Simeon told me to see their big brother Jaime (known to everyone as "Jim") instead of Juanito. Jim had just married Bertie Bernabe (another distant cousin of mine), and I had some trouble getting in touch with him, even though Simeon had told me where to find him. I finally got hold of him, fresh from his honeymoon, after a few attempts. After a short talk about families and such, I told him that I wanted to join his group.

As it turned out, his group, the ROTC Hunters, aimed to organize the men who had been ROTC students at all the Filipino colleges and universities. I was so intent on fighting the Japanese that I would have joined any group that would have me, even the Huks (Hukbalahaps)—the radical communist group. Though I was not yet even in college, Jim knew that I was kind of a gangster and was tough. He seemed very happy to learn that I wanted to join his group. He told me that my close cousin Pepe Lara was in charge of the forces in Don Galo and to report to him—and so I did.

Before I knew it, I was getting orders from almost everybody.

You must realize, of course, that we had to pretend that life goes on—that we were not actively opposing the Japanese. Soon, the schools reopened, and I started back to school. I played basketball, as always, and mahjong. All the while, though, the guerrillas were gearing up. Though I was the lowest of the low in the organization, I began receiving assignments even before my formal induction.

The first order of business was strictly police action, in the literal sense. When the Americans left and the Japanese took over all civic duties, ordinary law and order fell apart. Business was disrupted, and many people had nothing to do. People began putting their time into gambling. There were cockfights almost every day, craps and dice games, all kinds of cards, mahjong, and—for the women—a game similar to Bingo. Most working people worked only half days and the rest of the day was devoted to gambling. Those without jobs and without money for gambling resorted to crime. Crime was high and rising. The Japanese Occupation Forces could not and would not do anything about it. The Japanese did not seem to care. The guerrillas then took over.

My first assignment was to tell all gamblers in Don Galo that *sabong*—cockfighting—was to be tolerated only on Sundays and all other gambling was restricted to weekends only. That was the first time people became aware of the existence of the organized guerrilla men. People did not know who the guerrillas were, but they listened. Those who did not listen were reprimanded and punished. Crime went down, and people worked longer hours and made more money. They also had more time to spend with their families, and wives were much happier. As we began to bring order back to our town's life, most people loved what the guerrillas were doing.

Our main goal, though, was to get rid of the Japanese. We did not have the arms to do it ourselves, so we counted on Douglas MacArthur's promise, "I shall return." At the direction of both MacArthur and our President Quezon—who headed the commonwealth government-in-exile from America—we became a network of intelligence and sabotage. Paranaque become a center of the guerrilla movement—the ROTC Hunters soon had something like 30,000 members across the country. Since we were so close to Manila and to the air base, which the Japs had commandeered, and since our little town was surrounded by fields and jungle where guerrillas could hide, Paranaque was the perfect location for the guerrillas.

Sadly, the Japanese were not our only enemies. Some Filipinos collaborated with the Japanese, for money or to curry favor, by reporting on the underground movement. Many guerrillas were killed by the Japanese "*zona*" system. The Japanese would round up all the men and bring them to some central location. There, one of their Filipino spies, wearing a hood with a slit in it for the eyes, would stare at each person as the Japanese watched. The spy never spoke; he would nod silently if he knew you were a guerrilla, and you were taken away and killed right then, without trial.

The *zona* was always terrifying. At any hour of the day or night, the Japs would round us up and take us to the town plaza or other public place, and we—especially those of us who were, in fact, guilty—never knew whether that was the end for us. Sometimes the terror got to be too much for some people. During one *zona*, after he had been through this terror many times, one of my cousins felt sure he would be picked and executed. Believing he was about to die, he wanted to know who the spy was. He made a bold move, grabbing the hood and exposing the identity of our local spy. My cousin was shot dead right there. The exposed spy, one of our town mates, was protected by the Japanese, but the guerrillas took care of him anyway. He was found dead with his hood on.

That was the way we had to deal with pro-Japanese Filipinos. Some spies would just disappear, obviously taken by the guerrillas. Some pro-Japanese men were shot in public when they resisted the guerrilla's arrest.

When I had enough warning of the *zona*, I would hide, like climbing the ilang ilang to the roof of our house. Still, I went through many *zonas*. My life was probably saved because I had a boyish face and carried schoolbooks. How could I be a guerrilla? I was just a schoolboy, busy with basketball and girls.

You might think it strange that, in the midst of a war, with my life always in question, I was still interested in girls. If you think about it, though, it is not so odd. War has never been known to induce celibacy, for one thing—and I was, after all, in the heat of adolescence. Do not forget, either, that we were doing our best to keep normal life going along.

At the beginning of the Japanese occupation in early 1942, I noticed that Aning Mendoza had grown up to be a pretty young lady. I had known her forever—she was even a distant cousin. Our families had lived in the barrio of Don Galo for generations. Now I noticed that she was very attractive, even stunningly beautiful. I pursued her, and we "fell in love." It was really nothing but holding hands and a little kiss here and there.

With Naty Santos, it might have been more serious. Naty was from Baclaran, also a barrio of Paranaque, and she and I had been "sweethearts" in elementary school. Back then, I was her boyfriend, more than her being my girlfriend, as I remember it. We were really only good friends, but we liked each other and we were always together, sharing food and helping each other with school work. At our elementary school graduation, I had told her that I was going to school in Manila for intermediate school and wouldn't see her anymore—she would be going to school in Baclaran. I gave her a small goodbye kiss on her forehead.

When we met again, during the war, she did not know at first that it was I, for I had grown to 5' 9". But I knew her—though she had also grown, she was just as beautiful as when she was a young girl. After so many years, we still liked each other. The small glow of love, from so many years before, did not need much help to become a flame. Our "little romance" from years before was now for real. I was crazy about her.

She was very smart and was already making tons on money, doing business buying and selling—sugar and rice, I thought back then, but years later she told me that she made her real money in black market currency exchange. I saw her as much as I could. I called her my "B&B girl friend," and whenever we went out for a date, the "beauty and brains" usually picked up the tab.

We were seriously in love, and I considered marrying her. Though I was of marriageable age, by Filipino standards, I did not feel that I was ready. I was just a student, and I was not getting paid as a guerrilla, although it took plenty of my time and made other work impossible. I talked it over with my mother, and her response matched my thinking—that I should not get married since I could not support a family. Truthfully, she scolded me rather severely for even thinking about marriage, under the circumstances. Kaka Mando's family of six was already a part of the de Lara household, under my parent's care, and nobody wanted another dependent family around, especially at this time.

The war separated Naty and me, and by the time I saw her again, everything had changed.

I had revealed to my father and Kaka Mando, but no one else, that I had joined the guerrillas. My mother did not know that I was a guerrilla until over a year later, when I was going away for field training. I was the only guerrilla in my immediate family, but the rest were all guerrilla supporters.

From the first, my father was concerned about whether I was involved in any killings, especially of Filipinos. I told him that I was not involved in any killings and would never kill anybody with my own hands. The guerrillas had trigger men who took care of eliminating our Filipino enemies. We had strict orders not to kill Japanese soldiers, if we could help it, especially if and when they were in town. We did not want to bring the Japanese down on ourselves in force, for that would defeat our long-range purposes of laying the groundwork for MacArthur's return.

In the early going, my main work was to report Japanese movements, Japanese concentrations, and their strength of armaments, including types and number of air planes. Back then, I was to cover only the area of Paranaque and Nichols Air Base—which was now the Japanese Air Field. I was not to write down what I had observed, so memory was crucial. I was chosen for this work because the Japanese Air Field was next to my father's salt/fish operations and his farm, so I could observe what was going on in the airfield while pretending to be about my ordinary business on Amang's properties. Of course, often I had to go beyond that obvious cover, to get close enough to identify and count armaments. All this information had to be reported once a week on a routine basis or when any special activity needed the attention of people higher up than I.

The property of my father's closest to Nichols Field was his "*kaingin,*" the farm for fruits, vegetables, and chickens. I would take a young relative of ours who was staying with us, an eleven year old boy, to get some fruits, like mangoes and guavas. Then we would take the long way home, walking the perimeter of the air field. My "assistant," who had no idea that I was a guerrilla, questioned why we always took the long way home; I just told him I was crazy about airplanes.

Quite a few times, Japanese guards at the air field questioned why we were hanging around near the fence. I would just offer the guard some mangoes or other food, which would be happily accepted, and usually that led to the end of the questioning. My "assistant" and I looked like a couple of ragamuffins, really—we just wore old boxer shorts and worn-out, sleeveless T-shirts. We had no guns—we certainly did not look threatening. Eventually, some guards even looked forward to seeing us come by, bringing free fruit! Little did they know that their little benefactor was gathering intelligence that went to MacArthur in Australia.

Only once did I dare to engage directly in overt sabotage on my own. I had the approval of my superior, Romy de Jesus. Two of my gang mates from before the war were stealing tires and gasoline from a Japanese truck and car depot located in the barrio of Tambo, next to Don Galo. My friend Pareng Hiling had told me about it, and he asked me to stop them—because they were our friends, and we feared for their lives if the Japs caught them.

I went to see them, and they knew why I was there—Pareng Hiling had already tried to stop them. They knew that I was a guerrilla, so right away they promised not to ever steal again. I told them to get me two five-gallon cans of gasoline, ostensibly for our family car. They said, "No problem." I told them that I would need it the following night, and that Pareng Hiling would take us to pick it up in his *caratela*.

When we got to the depot the next night, I left Pareng Hiling in the *caratela* and went with the bandits to the depot. I told them not to bring the cans out to the *caratela*, but just to spill the gas all over and strike a match. They were surprised at my instructions but happy to comply. I went back to the *caratela*, and Pareng Hiling and I drove about a block away and stopped to wait. After awhile, we heard the explosion and saw a huge fire. Pareng Hiling was shocked, and I told him what I had done. He was very frightened, fearing the bandits would be caught and would "squeal." I had told them where to meet us, and they did not show up.

Pareng Hiling and I vamoosed. About fifty new trucks and some cars were all burned. Fearful that the two accomplices had been captured, I hid out in the guerrilla hideouts for several weeks just in case they implicated me. As it turned out, they had hidden safely that time—though they did not stop stealing and were later caught "red-handed" by the Japanese and killed.

Until early 1944, my further guerrilla activities mostly consisted of intelligence work and support for other activities of the guerrillas. Life as a guerrilla was dangerous enough without adding the terror of active sabotage.

Though the Philippines had essentially fallen to the Japanese in one day, MacArthur's withdrawal and the U.S. capitulation formally ended when General Wainwright—whom MacArthur had left behind when he departed to Australia—surrendered Corregidor on May 8, 1942. At last, everything was quiet. No more planes, no air raid sirens, and no blackouts. Many families that had fled Don Galo returned—including Stella's.

I was playing basketball one afternoon in front of our house, when I saw Stella for the first time in quite some time. This was probably in the summer, not long after her return. She was with a few of her friends, watching us play basketball. I suddenly noticed her in a way I never had before. Somehow she had managed to grow up—to a height of about 5' 6", with a very nice figure. She wasn't a skinny little girl anymore. She did not stay for very long and left before our game was over.

I went crazy thinking about the new Stella. I dropped, and completely ignored, my other girls and pursued her. But Stella would not even smile at me, although I knew she was friendly with others. She always had a ready smile, except for me. Whenever I saw her with her friends, I still would receive the same response. They all would return my friendly greetings, except Stella.

Stella was not shy, but very reserved. I sent her a love letter, telling her how much I liked her, but she did not respond. I followed it with two more letters, with the same results. I confronted one of her friends with whom I was very close—she was, in fact, my favorite dancing partner—and asked why Stella had been indifferent to me. She said that Stella just did not like me. Other friends that I asked, though, said they could not understand it—that Stella always wanted to hear everything about me, and that they thought she liked me.

This was agony! She would always join her friends whenever my team would be playing basketball in front of our house. All her friends would jump with joy and scream loudly whenever I scored a basket or intercepted a pass or blocked a shot. But I would look at her, and she would not have any reaction, as if she could not have cared less.

Life must go on, though, so I resumed pursuing other girls. Still, I did not give up pursuing Stella. I loved her music. She was beautiful. She was the kind of girl I had always dreamed of. I enjoyed listening to her piano playing and would hang around with my friends, in front of her house, to listen to her music.

I could not get Stella off my mind. I tried my very best to win her affections. I started dressing well, shaving regularly, and behaving properly, all to no avail. Whenever she saw me she would act as if I did not exist. I even went to one of her piano recitals. When I congratulated her afterwards, she just said, "Thank you," almost inaudibly, with a serious face and no smile. I watched how she would respond to others—they all received a sweet smile and heartfelt, "Thank you." My heart sank.

Coming home one afternoon after playing basketball, I heard somebody playing the *Warsaw Concerto* on the piano in our house. I wondered who it could be, since no one in our family could play so well. I did not think that it could be Stella, but to my surprise and delight it was she. She stopped playing when she saw me and greeted me with a sweet smile. I was shocked—happily shocked.

"Hello, Stella," I almost stammered. "Please don't stop. I want to listen."

Without saying a word, she nodded, smiled, and turned back to the piano. After playing for a few more minutes, she stopped and approached me. "I've been practicing for over two hours. That's enough for today. I will be giving a recital in a few days, but my piano at home is being tuned, so I asked your mother if I could practice here. She said, 'Yes,' and she even gave me a piece of cake."

I said to her, "Did you know that today was the first time, ever, that you have smiled at me? What have I done to deserve all this?"

She looked surprised, but she kept smiling. "Your behavior has changed." Maybe I looked disbelieving, but she became adamant as she said, "I always liked you. It was your behavior that I was not very particularly fond of."

I did not like her saying this. Perhaps, as the psychologists would say, I had a lot of self-esteem. Or maybe my pride was just hurt. She was right that my behavior had changed, due to my falling in love with her. But I did not want to admit it. I spoke sternly to her: "Listen, Stella, and remember. I have not changed and would never change anything in me. You take me the way I am, or we'd just as well remain the way we were, never speaking."

She looked shocked. "You are being rough on me. Let's change the subject."

I did not want to let it go. I was really very happy, but maybe I was just getting even for all the times she snubbed me. We bickered until it looked as if she would begin crying, so I gave in. I said, "You really have made me very happy today. Let's move to another subject, as you wished."

Her face brightened. "I heard you playing the Schubert *Serenade* on the piano yesterday. I want to give you some pointers."

"And how much are you going to charge me for those pointers?" I asked her.

"There will be no charge, as long as you are a good student," she said, with a coy smile.

"I will try," I said—and then, spontaneously, we hugged and kissed!

That was the start of our long affair, in about November of 1942. She showed me how to play Schubert's *Serenade* correctly, with emotion. She told me that if I really loved her, I would learn to play it that way and play it every time I was thinking of her.

And so I did. I played it many times a day. She also played our *Serenade* before she started her practice routine. Since we lived so close to each other, we could hear each other play—a sort of musical love letter each time. Neither of us suspected that this would be her funeral song.

During the war, I never told Stella that I was a guerrilla. Whenever I had to go to the field for guerrilla tactics training or other guerrilla missions, I would give her some excuse. Always, when I returned home, a few short messages from her would be waiting for me.

When I was home, we spent as much time together as possible. We spent many afternoons walking on the beach, doing what all lovers would do, while watching the romantic setting of the late afternoon sun. We spent countless hours together at my house and at hers, and she coached me tirelessly at the piano, especially to teach me the way Schubert's *Serenade* should be interpreted, a romantic, slow, loving music. For Valentine's Day, 1943, she wrote out her interpretation of the *Serenade*, with exact instructions on how it should be played. She also gave me a gold locket with her picture in it.

Of course, like all young lovers, we had our disagreements. Some were easy to settle—I had no problem wearing the kinds of clothes and hair styles she preferred. I think the only one of any consequence in those days was her dislike of my "gang," my Don Galo friends. She liked my Manila friends, but she wanted me to get rid of the Don Galo gang. Of course, I refused. Stella also disapproved of my gambling. At first, I agreed to give it up, but later I began gambling behind her back—going to play mahjong after leaving her in the evenings. I did give up cockfights more or less completely—for cockfights were held on Sundays, when I either had a basketball game or spent the day with Stella. She liked that I spent my free time on Sundays with her instead of in the *sabongan*.

Stella wasn't perfect, either. She was a very jealous person, for one thing. Since she did not like dancing, she had to learn to tolerate my love for it—which required that I have other girls as dancing partners. I can't say she ever got over her jealousy, but she did understand that if she wasn't going to dance with me, she should let other girls do it.

We never talked of marriage, in that first year. I was very clear that I was in no position to be married—that issue had gotten settled when I was in love with Naty. With the war and my inability to earn money, since my guerrilla work took so much time, the issue was not even on the agenda that first year.

The agenda changed, though.

Whenever I came home, I would ask everybody at home if they had heard Stella playing the *Serenade*—in fact, the question became so routine, I did not have to ask; they would just tell me, first thing, when I got home. One late evening, after a game of basketball, the news was that no one had heard the *Serenade* that day. I went around and double checked with everyone at home, but everyone had the same message. No *Serenade* that day. I was disappointed, but I didn't think it was a big deal. Maybe I should have known it was a big deal—she had never missed the *Serenade* even once before. It was already late at night, and the next day I had to leave early for school, so I did not go to see her until the afternoon of the following day. She met me and began crying uncontrollably, telling me that her uncle, a physician, had taken her to the hospital—she had been coughing, not too severely but persistently for a couple of weeks, and she had felt a little weaker than usual. She had not been very alarmed, nor had I—but at the hospital, she had learned she had tuberculosis, a very dreadful disease, almost certainly a death sentence during the war.

That hit me so hard. I was so devastated that I could not sleep nights. Why would it happen to the woman I love? I realized that I could not bear the thought of living without Stella.

She was fortunate that her uncle was an excellent medical doctor; she had first-rate care of the most attentive sort. For quite some time, she was bedridden, spending most of her time reading. The doctor had forbidden her to play the piano more than half an hour each day-a half-hour that always included our *Serenade*. She very seldom went out, except when going to the doctor or downstairs into her yard for fresh air and sun. She did her exercises, as prescribed, and ate exactly what her uncle told her to eat. She was frustrated that she had to suspend almost all of her normal activities. We had to suspend most of the things we normally did together. We could not even kiss, for her type of tuberculosis was highly contagious.

For awhile, she was so weak, and I was so busy with the guerrillas, that I saw her only once or twice a week. That was agony. I visited her at home whenever I could, but we also talked by using the hand signals I had learned as a boy scout. We did not have telephones—we had had them before the war, but they did not work during the war, when we certainly could have really used them.

Since we were neighbors, the distance between her window and mine was less than fifty feet. Our houses were diagonally opposite, separated by a street about twenty feet wide. It was close enough to read the hand signals but too far to carry on a verbal conversation. She had to learn the hand signals, of course. We got to be so proficient at it that we were usually able to communicate perfectly. Occasionally, we were not sure what each other had said, so we exchanged short notes to clarify. We did not hide from people the way we communicated. It was an open secret. All our neighbors knew of our affair and were amazed how well we could communicate. Her grandmother—a very traditional person who was not my biggest fan, anyway—did not approve completely of the unconventional way we were carrying on our relationship, so Stella would have to warn me when she was around.

Under her uncle's care, Stella's disease initially yielded completely, it seemed. Good food, rest, and continuous medication cleared all the dark spots in a matter of several weeks, according to the X-ray reports. We hoped she was now one of the rare ones who would survive—but the respite did not last long. Her disease followed a course of ups and downs. She would respond for awhile—and whenever a new medicine or nutritional regimen helped, she would be so happy and could not wait to tell me. I would go to her house and we would talk exuberantly about the future. We would resume some of our activities. Sometimes she seemed perfectly healthy, and we could do anything. Then her cough would come back, and she would weep, knowing what that meant.

Stella's illness gave great fervor to my guerrilla activities: Her uncle knew that new antibiotics, which cured TB, had been developed in America, but we could not get them during the war. I became a fanatic, working harder and harder as a guerrilla, for the Japanese to be defeated.

In Stella's illness, I realized the seriousness of my feelings for her, and so did my family. They had always been happy that Stella and I were involved; but now they knew that I loved her in a way that was different from anyone before. They supported that one hundred percent.

Stella's family also changed in their attitudes toward me during her illness, probably because they saw how much I loved her. Though they had always acted politely toward me—and I think her mother always liked me—the grandmother had been opposed to our romance, and her stepfather had maintained an inscrutable formality. (He was a politician, remember, so I never knew exactly what he really believed.) I had always gotten the feeling that the whole family looked forward to the day when Stella moved on to a more suitable companion—one with fewer bad habits and less troublesome friends. After Stella became ill, though, her mother and stepfather became much warmer to me. I was never entirely sure about the grandmother, but even she seemed less cool toward me. They all seemed to accept that Stella and I belonged to each other.

By now, it was late 1943-early 1944. MacArthur had begun winning substantial victories through the Pacific, and everyone knew it was a matter of time before he kept his promise, "I shall return." For one thing, he kept reminding us: He had cigarette packages, matches, and candies printed with that slogan and smuggled into the Philippines, everywhere, to keep people's spirits alive.

MacArthur's impending return was great for the country, but it had a serious downside for Stella and me. My guerrilla activities carried me further and further afield, as we had more duties—I will tell you about these soon—to help prepare for MacArthur's eventual invasion. Stella's family decided to leave Paranaque and go somewhere further from the capital, to avoid the fighting we all knew would be coming. Stella and her family moved to the outskirts of the town of Mandaluyong, three hours from Don Galo by *caratela,* though less than an hour by car. Just when I knew that I wanted to spend my life with Stella, the war separated us. I visited her as often as I possibly could, but now we had more dreams of the future than time together.

Chapter Four

Liberation

Throughout the war, the U.S. supported the guerrillas by smuggling in radios, food, cigarettes, medical supplies, and arms. In early 1944, the rate of smuggling increased, in preparation for an eventual invasion. The guerrillas needed as many men as possible to help with the smuggling. By now, I was nearly twenty years old, and I had proved myself through nearly three years of guerrilla activity. To my intelligence duties were added (among other things) field trips to bring in supplies.

We had to travel on foot from Paranaque to Infanta, in the western part of our island of Luzon. We would meet the American submarines under cover of night, unload the supplies, then transport and hide them—still on foot, for the most part—all without being caught by the Japanese.

Intelligence activities around Paranaque were dangerous enough, even though I could easily pretend to be about my ordinary business. Still, they were rarely all that uncomfortable. Outside Paranaque, the situation was different—much more dangerous and uncomfortable. As we walked the hills, we had to be very careful not to be discovered. We were armed, so we would not be able to pretend we were not guerrillas if we were caught. We had little food—if we ate one good meal in a four-day walk, we were lucky—and we had little or no shelter. I spent a great deal of time suffering from diarrhea, and I contracted malaria. The malaria stayed with me for years.

We carried arms to our guerrilla hideouts in the west coast and the central towns. We had to bring a large amount to our field hideout in Paranaque. On one trip, as we neared the fields of Paranaque, we ran into about a half-dozen Japanese soldiers on foot. We spotted them from about a thousand feet away. There were a couple dozen of us, all heavily armed. I was carrying two .45 caliber handguns and two carbines. We were ordered by our leader to spread out, deploy, and get ready to fire. The Japanese soldiers had spotted us, too—and ran away.

We hid until sundown, then continued our trip, depositing the arms in our field hideout, and heading home. I knew that Japanese guards, who had taken over my father's bakery as their headquarters and guard post, stood watch at the foot of the main Paranaque Bridge. Since I looked like a prime suspect for guerrilla activity—I had not bathed or shaven for days, and I was a big mess from walking and hiding in the woods—I knew it was dangerous to try to cross the bridge. I swam across the river to Santo Ninyo (formerly named Ibayo) and went home, once again, by way of my father's Ibayo Bridge.

The following day, probably because their soldiers who had spotted us had reported guerrilla activity in the area, the Japanese killed all men and boys in the fields of Paranaque, more than sixty innocent males.

As the hoped-for invasion came closer, the guerrillas had more and more work to do. Intelligence became ever more crucial; the Americans, and the Filipinos who would rise up with them, had to know exactly what we were up against. We had to know just who the Japanese collaborators were and where they were located, so that they could be "neutralized" when the invasion was imminent. We had to distribute our own arms and be sure we were well trained and ready to move into active warfare. Whenever possible, we had to free key Filipino leaders who had been captured, but not yet executed, by the Japanese.

When we had to break a political prisoner out of jail, we rarely had to fight, though we had to be prepared to fight. Usually, we could bribe a guard—even a Japanese guard—to let the prisoner "escape." We could not count on the cooperation of other Japs beside the corrupt guard. Always a group of the youngest and fittest of us stood ready while a senior guerrilla went forward to secure the prisoner. In the jailbreaks in which I was involved, we always managed to get away undetected, without firing a shot.

Not only were my activities from 1944 more dangerous and more physically demanding; the Japanese stepped up their attempts to root out the guerrillas, conducting more *zona*. Those of us who survived had become quite adept at hiding.

When I could, I tried to get to Mandaluyong to see Stella. Usually I had to borrow a *caratela*. Gasoline for the car was hard to get, but even worse, automobiles had to have permits from the Japanese, which were harder to get than gasoline. Twice, though, I managed to drive to Mandaluyong. The last of these trips, I thought I had taken the last trip of my life.

This must have been in the late summer of 1944. I planned the trip myself, asking six of her friends to come along. She always loved to see her friends, and I knew this would make her very happy. We left Don Galo early one morning, arriving in Mandaluyong only an hour later. We told jokes and stories, and we talked about what was going on in Don Galo and with other friends. I took her for a short ride in the car, and we parked and talked for about an hour. The friends and I left in the late afternoon, probably around five o'clock.

Unfortunately, we had a lot of car trouble. Probably the gasoline, which I had bought on the black market, had some water in it. Whatever the cause, the car would run a few miles, then stall out. Before too long, I had worn the battery out restarting the car, so whenever it stalled, we had to push the car to get it started.

At one point, almost to Paranaque, we were pushing the car and came to a Japanese sentry post. We stopped in front of the sentry to make our ninety-degree bows—something I had become quite careful always to do. One of the guards approached us to help us start the car with a jumper.

I had learned to speak Japanese passably well, so I was able to communicate with him. I thought he was really trying to help us—but then he checked our driving permit and discovered it was expired. He detained all of us, initially.

He demanded to see our resident certificates, which everyone was supposed to carry at all times. When I reached into my pocket to get it, my wallet was gone. I had no identification of any kind. I cannot tell you the panic that chilled my heart. If the Japanese did too much investigation to establish my identity, they might get some word that I was a guerrilla, and that would be the end of me.

My passengers, whose papers were in order, were released. They searched the car for my wallet but could not find it. I had told them to send word to Stella to see if I had left it at her place, and to tell my parents and Kaka Mando of my plight.

My family sent someone to Stella's place to look for the wallet. Meanwhile, my father and mother came to the sentry house and promised to get duplicates of my resident certificate and driver's license. All of that was well and good, but it did not address the problem of why I had been driving with an expired travel permit. The truth of the matter is that my trip to see Stella had been delayed so I could help break a political prisoner out of jail. I did not think the guards would accept that explanation very happily.

Stella found my wallet a day or two later, but that brought about problems of its own. My name and date of birth were not consistent. My resident certificate had my name as Rudolfo de Lara, born 1926, while my driver's license had the name was Rodolfo Lara ('de' was omitted), born 1922. We had to explain that, before the war, I had lied about my age to get my driver's license years earlier than was really legal. We had to convince them that the discrepancies in name meant nothing, that omitting the "de" was common practice, and "Rudolfo" and "Rodolfo" were really the same name.

There was still the problem of the expired travel permit. Kaka Mando came to the rescue. He was a smooth talker and very charming. He could have told the Japanese that he owned the Paranaque Bridge, and they would have believed him. Kaka Mando risked his life by swearing out a statement that I had just failed to make the trip within the allocated dates because of car trouble, and that I had not even realized the permit was expired—the permit was written in Japanese Hirigana (Chinese) characters, instead of the Katakana that I understood.

The Japanese did not treat me badly during the six days I was under arrest. They liked the fact that I was communicating with them in Japanese, I think, and they probably believed all along that I was a wayward schoolboy who had been out on a lark with his friends. They fed me well enough—rice and dried fish, with plenty of water, three times a day. Still, the sheer terror that they would find out the truth kept me awake the entire time I was detained.

Not long after that, late in the summer of 1944, the Japanese informed us that they would be taking our house in Don Galo for storage and officers quarters. We had to vacate in a hurry. By now, no one doubted that MacArthur would be returning, and our family, except for me, headed for the town of Obando, in the Bulacan province, north of Manila, for safety. I stayed with Pareng Hiling and his wife and child, who lived in a small rental house that my father owned, and in the guerrillas' field hideouts. Until the invasion actually came, I saw my family regularly—Amang and Inang would come to Don Galo on Sunday nights to pick up money their businesses had earned during the week, and I would go to visit them in Obando.

The Japanese had no intention of surrendering to MacArthur, and they stepped up their efforts to root out any spies or other guerrillas who might help him when the invasion came. While my family was in Obando, they went through many *zonas*—for some of them, I happened to be there.

The very-old Spanish house that my family rented in Obando had a water-storage tank to collect water that drained from the roof during rainy days. Essentially a big box made of reinforced concrete, it was about twelve feet wide, twenty feet long, and twelve feet deep, with an opening in the roof about three feet in diameter. Amang made the tank into a place for hiding during the *zonas*, installing custom-made benches inside, just above water level. Whenever warning of a *zona* reached the house, all the men headed for the tank. The Japs never figured out the hiding place. Once, when I was there, a Jap soldier looked through the opening in the roof, and we thought we were done for. But when he saw that the water was quiet and still, he must have decided that nobody could be inside. He left.

Many innocent males and guilty guerrillas were killed on those *zonas* in Obando. In the last of them, the father of my friend Pilar (who would later be a girlfriend) went missing. After he was gone for a number of days, Pilar and her mother went to the killing field, where bodies of victims were all piled up. Pilar saw familiar feet and trousers near the bottom of the pile. She and her mother began wailing and crying, and they ran home to tell what they saw. When they entered the house, they saw a ghost—the ghost of Pilar's father. At least, that's what they thought. Her father quickly explained that they must have mistaken another body for his, because he had just come out from hiding in next town.

General MacArthur landed in Leyte, an island fairly far south of Luzon, on December 7, 1944. He battled for over two months to capture Leyte—we could keep up with war news on the shortwave radio the Americans had provided for our guerrilla headquarters. He then took over the island of Mindoro, just southwest of Luzon, to use as a staging area for his great campaign to free Luzon, the main island of our country. On January 9, he launched the second-largest offensive of the entire war, leading 300,000 soldiers, both American and Filipino, regular soldiers and guerrillas, against the Japanese on Luzon.

MacArthur made a big deal of wanting to celebrate his sixty-fifth birthday in Manila on January 26, 1945. That did not happen. We heard on our short wave radio that the *Newsweek* headlines of February 12, 1945 said: "The prize of the Pacific War—Manila—fell to General Douglas MacArthur like a ripened plum." Even that date is not really true. The Japanese fought to the last man, up until March 29, 1945.

When MacArthur invaded Luzon, the guerrillas became full-fledged fighting units. With ten or twelve of my compatriots, I was dispatched to Infanta, where we met other guerrillas and were attached to the U.S. Eleventh Airborne.

We headed for Manila, with U.S. artillery tanks leading our convoy and observation planes above. U.S. fighter jet planes flew low, back and forth, clearing our way. The Japanese fled the out-lying areas, concentrating in Manila and Nichols Air Base. We entered Paranaque without firing a shot; on February 4, 1945, we entered Don Galo.

Captain Romeo de Jesus, with about twenty of us, was assigned to remain in Don Galo and defend the barrio against Japanese snipers and renegades—and to keep an eye on the activities at Nichols Air Base.

As soon as I could, I went to our house in Don Galo to see if it had withstood the rigors of the fighting. It was damaged—some holes in the roof—but structurally sound.

The occupants of the house had fled so quickly that they had left a pot of newly-cooked rice, untouched, on the stove. In the garage I found two cars—an old Plymouth sedan and a Hudson that had been made into a pick-up truck. This was a boon—we had gotten rid of the family car shortly after my detention by the Japanese authorities. Almost as exciting, the second floor was full of sacks of rice, stacked about three or four feet high. There were hundreds and hundreds of sacks of white rice. I said to myself, "Man, I'm a rich boy."

I had to get out of the house, for a few Japanese soldiers still prowled the streets of Don Galo, retreating, but armed and fighting, with no thoughts of surrender. I was carrying a .45 semi-automatic handgun and a carbine. I locked the main door and secured the whole house. While I was locking the front gate, a man I hardly knew, who could hardly walk, asked if there was anything in our house to eat. He appeared to be malnourished and bloated for lack of food. I felt sorry for him, so I went back upstairs and got him a small amount of rice—maybe five or ten pounds, which was all he could carry in his sad state.

I then left to get my father, who had been trapped in Don Galo when the fighting broke out and was staying in his salt warehouse. The first thing I told my father when I saw him was that I had a house full of rice.

I did not tell him that I had started scheming about how to sell the rice. I decided to enlist the help of the guerrillas. That night, I met with my cousin, Pepe Lara, and he, Romy de Jesus, and three other guerrillas agreed to do the job. We also agreed that the guerrillas would take the Plymouth sedan and the Hudson would be mine.

The next day, when I took my father to inspect our house, I was shocked that the rice was all gone—I never thought my compatriots would be so quick and efficient! I told my father the truth about selling the rice. He was, we can say, not entirely happy at the idea of my profiteering.

As it turned out, my compatriots and I had been double-crossed by the men they enlisted to help sell the rice, and we got very little of money from the sale. I was so angry! But Amang would not tolerate that. He taught me a very important lesson. He told me sternly, "You did not earn it, so you did not deserve it." He reminded me that not only did I not deserve it, I did not even need it, unlike so many people who had nothing.

I look back on this episode with great shame. I should not have been so greedy; I should have given the rice to the poor people for free. I have never forgotten my father's admonitions on that day.

This was a very strange time. On the one hand, we had taken Don Galo so easily, and we faced no organized Japanese opposition once we were there. On the other, fighting in Manilla, so nearby, was vicious. The Japanese were wantonly raping and murdering civilians, as well as fighting the Americans for all they were worth. Meanwhile, the U.S. had set up artillery batteries just south of Don Galo, in the barrio of San Dionisio, to bombard Nichols, and the Japs were bombarding back. Since Don Galo was right in the middle, many wayward shells fell into the town. Amang and I were in Don Galo, while our family was up north, unreachable because of the terrible events in and around Manila. We were home, but not really, and safe, but not really.

Among the strange things about this time, Amang and I really had so much fun together, more than we had enjoyed together since those childhood walks on the beach.

I was working very hard on my Hudson pickup truck, getting ready to get our family from Obando and, for sure, to go see Stella. I had the engine running perfectly well, like a Buick, but the transmission needed a new clutch. The clutch on this odd car was made of cork—the same material used to stopper wine bottles. Such a thing was nowhere to be found. I tried making a clutch from the rubber from old tires, or from pounded coconut husks glued together, or hundreds of wine bottle corks glued together. Every time, my improvised clutch would work for awhile and then fall apart.

Amang worked hard patching the roof of our house and also the bakery roof. I told him that I could get him plenty of work patching roofs in Paranaque. He did not think it was funny, for he was already sixty-five years old.

Amang cooked for the two of us this whole time. When the war broke out, our maids from the north had all gone home, and the young married couple who worked for us during the war was in Obando with our family. Honestly, Amang was not the best cook in the world. I doubt if he had ever cooked before in his life. I had never seen him in the kitchen before except when he was hungry and would pick at whatever food Inang was cooking until Inang would drive him out of the kitchen.

The first meal he cooked for us was so bland. Though he was a salt merchant, with a salt warehouse full to the roof, he used no salt at all in our first meal together. I enjoyed eating that meal anyway, because I was starving and I was so intent on my conversation with Amang. That initial tolerance for his bad cooking wore off.

At one meal, when he was in a good mood, I asked him how long he and Inang had been married. He asked me why I wanted to know. I told him, "My question calls for an answer, not for another question." He looked at me sort of funny, but he told me how long they had been married. I asked him if that included living together before they got married—a question he did not appreciate. I don't think he spoke much to me that day.

I picked up the topic again when we had lunch together the next day. First, I gave him a nice compliment, saying that his cooking had improved. He asked me, in a very unusually low voice, what I meant by "improved." I said that since he had been married to Inang for about a hundred years, he should be cooking as well as Inang. He did not like that at all. He said, "I earn the money and Inang cooks the food." I said that was a nice excuse, and I don't think he liked that, too.

Our menu improved when life in Don Galo began to get back to normal, with vendors going door to door, carrying fruits and vegetables in flat baskets on the tops of the their heads. Amang was their best customer.

The guerrillas established our local headquarters at the home of Maxima Bernabe, just across from my father's bakery on the main street of Paranaque (now called Quirino Avenue).

On about February 6, 1945, the U.S. Army's Eleventh Airborne Unit deposited belongings of dead soldiers in Don Galo Barrio Chapel. They were in the process of sorting the belongings when I identified myself as a guerrilla. I told the officer in charge about Stella's tuberculosis, and he gave me many first-aid supplies and medicines. I was really after antibiotics, especially the new drug penicillin that I had just recently heard about—but he had none.

That evening, I stayed with the family of Brihita and Bankoy Agustin. They owned and operated a *sari-sari* (sell-all) store. They were my friends; I had often spent evenings with them. I sorted two big bags of drugs I had gotten earlier in the day. I had aspirins, sulfalinamide, and many sulfa drugs. I tried to study which drug was for what. I also had two containers of dried blood plasma.

The Agustins' sari-sari store faced the compound of Paranaque's mayor, Dr. Juan Gabriel—Dr. Juan, as he liked to be called. Dr. Juan's home, which was unoccupied at the time, was at the rear of the compound, facing the Paranaque River. The house was beautiful, a semi-concrete, contemporary home. There was also a rice warehouse within the compound, with a bomb shelter built under it. Not quite at the center of the compound, but nearer to Dr. Juan's house, a big tree offered shade.

Late in the afternoon, a stray bullet wounded one of the Agustins' pigs. The Agustins decided to slaughter it, but to wait until morning.

Cannon shells from the Japanese and the Americans continued all night long, around the clock. In the early morning, the fireworks coming from the Japanese air base died away—only shells from the Americans were flying over our heads. We figured that the enemy ran out of ammunition, and since the Americans were very accurate with their shots, this would be the safest time to slaughter the pig.

None of us had ever undertaken such an enterprise before. The toughest question was, who would kill the pig? There were six of us, and the three females could not and would not do it. The third male was a two-year-old boy. The choice as to who would be the assassin was really only between Bankoy and me. I told them that I would do everything else, but not the killing of the poor pig. I had never even killed a chicken!

Bankoy suggested that we flip a coin. I said okay, but I swore that if I lost, I would use my handgun, never a knife, to kill the sow. I was really serious about it, so the women pleaded with Bankoy, who then unwillingly gave in and decided to do it. (Shooting the pig, rather than slitting his throat, would waste some meat.)

We decided to kill the pig in Dr. Juan's yard, then clean it on a big table under the shade tree. The women and I boiled the water for the cleaning, while Bankoy dispatched the pig. None of us even looked to see how Bankoy did it. We heard the pig give out several loud screams, then go silent. Bankoy asked me to help him put the poor thing on top of the table.

All six of us were seated on two long benches around the long table, cleaning the pig, when a stray shell from the Japanese artillery hit our table. The blast was so loud and strong that we were all thrown to the ground. At first, I could see nothing, as if the place were in total darkness. My ears were ringing, and I could hardly hear the crying and the screaming around me. As I gathered my senses, coughing and groping through the thick dust, I searched my whole body with my hands for any wound or injury. I was unscathed. Around me, though, my companions were crying and in pain. I told everyone to run to the other side of the Dr. Juan's house, the side away from the Japanese, and toward the U.S. troops.

When we got there, I began examining everyone. Brihita had small wounds on her leg and arm. In her arms, she held her son, still and quiet—a piece of steel shrapnel lodged in his chest, in front of his heart. I grabbed for the shrapnel and burned my hands—all of this must have taken only seconds, for the steel was still so hot. While I was searching for something to protect my fingers, Brihita told me not to bother—the boy was no longer breathing. I felt the boy's pulse; he was gone. He had saved his mother's life, for had the shrapnel not taken him, it would surely have taken her.

I asked Bankoy to get some clean towels or clothes to dress wounds. The lady visiting the Agustins, whose name I cannot now remember, had a deep wound in her upper arm, and it was bleeding profusely. She begged me to help her. Bankoy handed me a bunch of diapers and my medicine bag. I tied a diaper over the wound to stop the bleeding and desperately searched for the sulfalinamide. Amidst all the sobbing and crying, I found the bottle that I thought contained the drug I wanted. I applied a few drops to the wound and wrapped it with a clean diaper. I gave the lady some of the medicine and told her to apply it and change the bandage regularly. I then attended to all the others, using the same procedure. Later, when the chaos had died down, I discovered I had grabbed the wrong bottle. I had dressed everyone's wounds with medicine for athlete's foot. Nonetheless, within a few days, all the wounds had healed.

We buried the young boy in the back yard of Dr. Juan's house. It was a very sad day.

My father came running in a little later, having heard that I was among the injured. He was so relieved upon learning that I was not hurt. My ears kept ringing the rest of the day, though.

When we had calmed down, we decided we might as well finish butchering the pig—but we could not find him. We looked all around, and we were about to conclude that he had miraculously disappeared. We gave up looking for the prize pig, but then my father spotted something way up in the top of the tree. It was the tattered body of the pig. My father said that the pig must have taken the direct hit, thus saving lives—particularly mine, for I had been seated in front of the pig.

Since few people in Paranaque knew how to drive, and even fewer in the guerrillas, I was basically the driver of the Plymouth during guerrilla activities that required it. However, on the morning of February 8, 1945, two days after the death of the pig and the young boy, Pareng Tangol, our group leader and my superior, ordered me to turn over the keys. I asked him who gave the order—I probably would not have given up the keys just because Tangol said so. He responded that it was his order—but he proceeded, nervously, to give me too many explanations and too many jokes about them, and I realized he was keeping something from me. From the way he was acting, I figured that the order must be some sort of secret that had come down from Jim Ferrer or someone else high up in the ranks of the Hunters. I said O.K. and handed him the keys.

Around four o'clock that afternoon, while I was at home with my father, an order came to help the designated driver of the car learn how to operate it properly. I asked, "Why not just use me as the driver?" I was told that they were going to a top-secret mission, with strict instructions to take only people from an approved list, which did not include me. Besides, they said, it was a very dangerous assignment.

That was fine with me—I had just been curious why they wanted to train a new driver when they already had me. I was not really that interested in joining them, preferring to stay home with my father. We had so much to talk about, and I could not remember the last time I had been alone with him in a calm atmosphere.

But then I heard one of the guerrillas say that they were going to the town of Imus, in the province of Cavite. I got so excited, for Stella and her family had recently moved there. Since I had found out that Stella had moved to Imus, I had always wanted to go see her there. At this point, I had not been able to see her for about six months.

I told Tangol that he'd better tell Justo—Jim Ferrer—that I wanted to be the driver, and that he ought to use me since I knew the car better than any one else. One of the group took the message, presumably to Justo, but came back with a negative response. I would not be allowed to join them, for reasons beyond my right to know. The messenger still would not tell me the top-secret purpose of the trip.

Then I asked permission to join only so far as Imus—they could leave me there, go about their business, then pick me up. Again the response was the negative.

But darkness was approaching, and the new driver could not figure out how to keep the car running—it had manual carburetion, which required a skilled hand on the choke, and the new driver just could not get the hang of it. Finally, someone sent the order to use me as the driver, all the way through—not just to Imus.

I did, in fact, get to see Stella in Imus, but our mission allowed me only a few minutes with her. When I saw her, I was shocked. Her tuberculosis was the worst it had ever been, and she was terribly thin and pale. As if that were not sad enough, I had to tell her that their house in Don Galo had been destroyed, so they could not return to it. The leader of our guerrilla squad cut the conversation short, saying it was time to head out to complete the mission. I will tell you about that mission, which led to my trial for murder, a little later. Stella and I did not even have time to talk about where her family might go. She promised to let me know where they would be moving, as soon as her parents decided. Though I was so happy to have seen her, I left feeling very bad about her condition and the uncertainty of when we would meet again.

By this time—the second week in February, 1945—the Philippine-American forces had surrounded Manila. The remaining Japanese forces would not give up. Admiral Iwabuchi, the famous naval officer, ordered his 20,000 men to fight to the death for the Emperor, but to be sure that their deaths were paid for in enemy lives. He distributed to his men alcohol confiscated from stores, shops and warehouses. The men turned into a drunken, raging mob. With a desperate, avenging fury, they launched an orgy of burning, shooting, raping, and torture. Young girls and women of all ages were raped, then beheaded. Men's bodies were hung in the air and mutilated. Babies' eyeballs were ripped out and smeared across the walls. Hospital patients were tied to their beds and the hospital torched. Admiral Iwabuchi did nothing to stop the nightmare, apparently even encouraging his men to do it. The Philippine-American forces struggled to root out the fanatic Japanese sailors, engaging them to hand-to-hand combat, from building to building throughout Manila.

Finally, the remaining survivors retreated to the walled city of Intramuros, where every one of them died fighting, including Admiral Iwabuchi. Over 60,000 (some say over 100,000) Filipino men, women, and children lay dead in Manila. General MacArthur said that the atrocities committed by Admiral Iwabuchi and his men would long be remembered as the most tragic and heinous incidents in the annals of "civilized" warfare.

On March 29, 1945, Manila was finally silent.

I remember that date very well, for my father and I had been anxiously awaiting the day when we could bring our family home. Don Galo people who had evacuated southward began returning to our barrio by early March, 1945, but those who had evacuated northward could not come home until Manila was pacified. On March 30, 1945, my father and I knew we could bring our family home.

We had heard no news from them since early February. Amang talked all the time about his worries over whether the family was all OK. I knew—though I did not tell Amang—that Jap soldiers were retreating through Obando, going to join General Yamashita in his new headquarters a couple of hundred miles north, in Baguio. They were raping women and slaughtering civilians as they went. I was worried, too, and I wanted to see the family—and I was dying for Inang's cooking.

Though Manila was quiet, at first I could not find a *caratela* whose driver was willing to go thru Manila. The Plymouth I had given to the guerrillas had been wrecked, and my "new" Hudson was not yet running—besides, getting gas was not possible. Fortunately, Pareng Hiling had just come back from evacuation with his family. Pareng Hiling had worked as a *kutsero* since he had gotten married, early in the Japanese occupation. His father had given him the *caratela* and a fast, strong horse called "Scurro." Scurro had saved Pareng Hiling's life during the war, when the Japanese were about to put him to death for stealing. Pareng Hiling freed himself, climbed over a fence, ran home, and rode Scurro—bareback—to the fields, where he hid safely. Pareng Hiling had the courage and the horse to get through to Obando. He offered to take me to get my family.

We left for Obando on March 30. I left my father home, for there were still dangers, with Japanese suicide groups and renegades roaming the countryside. Besides, I needed all the space in the *caratela* for the large family—my mother, two sisters, two brothers, my brother's family of five, two servants, and all the personal belongings.

As we headed north, we debated which route to take. There were three ways to go through Manila to Obando. Dewey Boulevard, next to Manila Bay, was nice and the street was wide, but it went directly to Intramuros, where the Japanese had all died fighting—we hoped. The second route was the continuation of the Paranaque's Quirino Avenue, which turned into Harrison Street in Pasay City. This street led just east of Intramuros. The third route, Taft Avenue, took us furthest from Intramuros. Pareng Hiling wanted to take Harrison, but I argued for taking Taft. I knew more about what was going on in Manila than my compadre, for I was following the situation closely. Plenty of Jap stragglers and renegades were on the loose and out for vengeance.

We started off on Taft. Still, Pareng Hiling was not one to give in easily. When we would meet another *caratela*, Pareng Hiling would shout at them, asking if there were Japs where they were coming from. Some said yes, and some said they did not know but had heard shots. Understanding these shouted conversations was nearly impossible, but Pareng Hiling would get some idea that one or another of them knew something, so he would turn around to follow whichever drivers seemed to know the most.

We could hear shots from far away, and most buildings and houses along Taft Avenue were severely damaged or burned to the ground—including a house that my father had given to Kaka Mando. He had never even gotten to live in that house, since it was very near the air base. The sight of the burned buildings and the sound of gunfire made the atmosphere very foreboding. Still, we kept going.

At one point, we saw about five *caratelas* parked to rest and feed the horses. Pareng Hiling did the same thing and gave Scurro a pale of water with oat bran and molasses. The people in two *caratelas* coming from Manila said that if we had weak stomachs, we should forget about going to Obando. They said the atrocities, which were not over, had left horrible sights. Pareng Hiling seemed to know one of the *kutseros*, who advised us to postpone our trip for at least a few days.

We talked for a long while whether to proceed or not. We were both worried about the possibility of encountering some Japanese. We were not armed and felt defenseless. But I feared for my mother and the rest of our family, and I didn't think Amang could stand even one extra day of anxiety. I told Pareng Hiling that I would like to go ahead. Without a word, he just gave Scurro a little "tsik-tsik" sound, telling the horse to go—and away we went.

We kept encountering people who advised us to turn back. By now, we had turned around so many times and taken so much advice, we were lost. Soon enough we found something to guide us—the smell of rotting flesh. The closer we got to Manila, the stronger the smell became. In the middle of the morning, as we approached the Quiapo Bridge into Manila, we saw piles of dead bodies, pushed to the edge of the road to make the street passable.

The bridge, damaged by bombs, was not passable. We were told that none of three major bridges—Santa Cruz, Jones, and Quiapo—were passable. We were told to go east towards Pandacan. We did, and we found that we could carefully cross the concrete Pandacan Bridge, though it had plenty of holes in it. The smell of dead bodies had not diminished.

We took the very long way to go to Obando. We went through Balintawak, through Polo, Maycawayan, and two or three more towns before we reached Obando. We were in Balintawak—about six miles north of Manila—when the obnoxious odor finally disappeared. We were very tired, but not hungry, when we finally reached my family late in the afternoon. Though Pareng Hiling's wife had packed some steamed rice, dried fish, and a bucket of water, I did not eat much all day, for the odor of dead bodies soaked my lungs and, more important, my mind.

When we finally reached my family's house late in the afternoon, nobody was home. None of the immediate neighbors were around. The people in the next block said that my family might be among those who had left a week earlier, fearing the savagery of the retreating Japanese soldiers. I didn't know what to do. I wanted to go look for the family at Kaka Mando's in-laws in northern Obando. Pareng Hiling brought out the rest of the food his wife had prepared, and we sat in the yard wondering how to proceed. As we sat there, Kaka Mando came into the yard with his kids and our little brother, Tommy. I jumped up and shouted, asking where were Inang and the others. Kaka Mando said they were not far behind.

When Inang and the others came into the yard, I shouted, "Amang is fine—I left him on top of the bakery roof, patching holes." They were happy and excited to see us—and we all laughed at the idea of Amang, at sixty-five, working on the roof.

After we greeted each other, they told me they had fled, taking a long journey on foot, to avoid the Japanese forces. They had not seen the Japs, but they had seen the Americans.

You remember that I told you Kaka Mando had vowed that the first American liberator his new-born son laid eyes on would be the child's godfather. While the family was avoiding the Japanese, the boy found his American. In the next town over from Obando, they saw two American soldiers, and Kaka Mando flagged them down. He explained to the first one that he must be the child's godfather. The soldier said he could not, for he was Jewish. The second soldier, though, was Corporal Edward Wadarsky, a Catholic of Polish ancestry. Wadarsky agreed, with joy and pride, and they immediately found a priest and set up the christening. You must understand that for Filipinos, the role of godfather is very important—the godfather becomes quite seriously part of the family. Edward Wadarsky became part of ours.

Pareng Hiling and I stayed for a day. We hired another *caratela* to help carry the load back to Don Galo. I assured Inang that there was no danger from the Japanese, though in truth, there were still a few Japanese snipers and saboteurs hiding around Manila. I just did not want her worrying, and we wanted the family home. I did not mention the dead bodies and the bad odor in the air.

We went back to Don Galo by a more direct route, crossing the Ayala Bridge to Ayala Boulevard to Taft Avenue, on into Don Galo. We saw so many dead bodies, and by now the stench was even worse. We were almost all sick and vomiting from the horror.

We reached home about two o'clock in the afternoon on April 1. My father stood in the yard, crying for joy, speechless. He hugged my mother and everybody else—except me—without saying a word, still crying. I said, "Amang, aren't you happy to see me? I love to be hugged." He said sternly, "No! I am not going to hug you. You did not take me along, and you kept me here alone in suspense." I said, "Oh, I thought you could no longer talk." That broke the deep mood. Everyone laughed.

Though the war was not quite over, Don Galo was peaceful, and we were confident that we and the Americans would never again lose the Philippines. We began rebuilding our house and repairing my father's businesses. Within a month, we had things in acceptable order, though it would take a year to get everything back as it was before the war.

We were very happy to be home, but our happiness was tempered with sorrow. Hundreds of thousands of Filipinos died during World War II. Some Filipinos joined the U.S. Armed Forces, fought the invading Japanese forces, and lost their lives. Over three-quarters of the casualties were civilians, however. Some were killed in Japanese bombing during the early stage of the war, and many were victims of U.S. bombing during the process of liberating the Philippines from the Japanese. Many died of malnutrition and illness. A relatively small number were Japanese collaborators, killed by the guerrillas. Most, though, died directly at the hands of the Japanese troops, whether in the *zonas* or the atrocious slaughter that marked their rule and their defeat.

None of us guerrillas kidded ourselves: We knew we could never have defeated the Japanese ourselves. We kept our country's hopes alive when the U.S. had been defeated, though. We kept some measure of order among the people, and we laid the groundwork for MacArthur's return. Though I was lowest of the low in the ROTC Hunters, and I kept my promise never to kill anyone by my own hand, I like to believe I played some small role in the freedom our country came to enjoy.

I knew that the Americans had kept my country from a fate worse than death by defeating the Japanese. My pro-American sentiments, always strong, now soared. Soon, Stella and I would be making our own plans to go to America.

Chapter Five

Kidnapped

During 1945, as we busily recovered from the Japanese occupation, the U.S. helped us both directly and indirectly. We received many medical supplies—my malaria really came under control only now, with U.S. medical care—food, and other materials. We also had many "luxury" goods on the black market—U.S. soldiers would steal from their posts and sell U.S. goods to Filipinos. To this day, Filipinos have special fondness for things like American cheese and candies that we first tasted from the black market.

We were rapidly approaching our country's full-fledged independence, which the U.S. had scheduled to grant us on July 4, 1946. For the first time in several years, we were hopeful and excited about the future.

My father's bakery, no longer serving as a Japanese guard post, had plenty of holes and some minor structural difficulties to be repaired.

Damage to the large, dome-shaped brick oven was more serious. The oven had to be completely rebuilt, and that would take several weeks, maybe months, since bricks were hard to get.

Kaka Mando's new American compadre, Corporal Edward Wadarsky, had become part of our family since becoming the godfather of Kaka Mando's son. He was a tall, slender fellow who liked to drink, though he rarely got really drunk. He suggested that, while waiting for bricks to repair the oven, my father open a bar and restaurant in the bakery building. As he pointed out, lots of American soldiers were now stationed in our area, and they had money to spend and needed a place to enjoy themselves.

My father thought that was an excellent idea. With help from Wadarsky and Kaka Mando, he had the place open within weeks. Called simply "B & R Place," it was a big hit right from the start. That certainly makes sense—these soldiers had just survived one of the biggest, most savage campaigns of the war, and R&R at "B&R" must have seemed like Heaven to them.

Besides food and drink, the place offered music—a piano and a small live band. With Corporal Wadarsky's guidance, my father concocted a cocktail, called "Kikapoo Juice," that became very popular with the G.I.'s. The drink was a mix of *lambanoug*, orange juice, a little sugar, *calamanci*, and a dash of hot sauce—*lambanoug* is a hundred thirty-proof native liquor, and *calamanci* is a very sour native lemon. The ingredients were very, very cheap, so my father made a huge profit on every glass of Kikapoo Juice. The place was open twenty-four hours a day, and G.I.'s came by the hundreds. "B & R Place" had to be expanded into an indoor-and-outdoor place, with tables all around the grounds, to accommodate them. My father raked in the money.

Both black and white soldiers patronized the place. That was the first time I had witnessed how bad and low the blacks were treated by the whites. I was really shocked. The soldiers were always getting into fights, usually whites fighting blacks—racial fights. There were actually shootings. That was the how my sympathy for blacks got started. You will understand the significance of that later on, when I tell you about my first marriage.

Ed Wadarsky spent a lot of time with us, at home and (even more) in "B&R Place." Between my pro-American sympathies and my talks with him about life in America, I made up my mind to head for the U.S. as soon as possible. The U.S. Navy accepted Filipinos as servicemen, and I knew of several who had joined. Wadarsky told me that was not the best idea. He said that if I really wanted to live in America, I had to have an education. Just joining the Navy would not really help me have a decent life once I got out and tried to live in America. He insisted I needed to get a college education—and if at all possible, I should go to an American college. He promised to help me with research about American schools, once he went home.

Stella and I had begun talking of marriage and a life together in America—though she was still living in Imus, I went to see her fairly often. She had finally gotten antibiotics and made another of her miraculous recoveries. Her recovery pleased all of us, but I remained guarded in my optimism; I had seen too many relapses following these recoveries to be entirely hopeful. Like Wadarsky, she was adamantly opposed to the Navy idea, though for reasons of her own—she wanted me safe at home. She insisted that I needed to go to a Filipino college for awhile to get a good enough record to apply to U.S. schools. (I had finished high school during the war, but we knew that would not be enough to get me into an American college.) She wanted to be a concert pianist in America, and we thought that we could both get there eventually. She just did not want me going away, ahead of her.

We actually argued seriously about this issue—I really wanted to join the U.S. Navy and go to America right away, and to have her join me as soon as possible. When her health took another sudden downturn, I changed my tune—I decided I could not leave her, that I would stay and go to college in the Philippines until she got well enough for us to go to America together. It is strange, I think, that her illness finally decided the issue of whether I would go to college or the Navy. Because of Stella's illness, I became a student instead of a seaman. My entire life has gone differently because of that.

I was in "B&R Place" with Ed Wadarsky in the afternoon of August 6, 1945, when we heard the news of the atom bomb being dropped on Hiroshima. We were ecstatic, knowing the war was about to be over, really over. In the early evening, G.I.'s began packing "B&R Place" to celebrate. The celebration got out of hand, with much drunken fighting. Shortly after midnight, there was a shooting outside the bar, and my father closed the place down.

That was the beginning of the end for "B&R Place." My father could not tolerate the violence and ugliness. Within a month or so, he shut it down forever, at the peak of its popularity and profitability. He devoted his attention to getting the oven fixed, and he reopened the bakery. The bakery brought in less money than "B&R Place," but my father said he was able to sleep better and live happier, without feelings of guilt about the bad things that soldiers did at "B&R."

Though we were making rapid progress toward recovery and freedom, order had not been completely restored. The guerrillas were no longer operative, the Jap police no longer existed, and the transition into a new political order had not been completed. People of low character had plenty of chances for criminal activities. Remember, too, that the Americans had not been in power long enough, before the war, to root out completely the long tradition of corruption the Philippines had developed under the Spaniards.

One day shortly after my father reopened the bakery—this must have been in early January, 1946—one of his new employees, a fellow named Kadio, told me he had a message for me from Stella. I thought that was a little odd, since she usually wrote me notes, but I didn't think much about it—communications were still difficult, with no phones and no reliable postal service. He said that Stella's family was moving to the town of Las Pinas, just next to Paranaque, to a house behind the Las Pinas Restaurant, and I should meet her at that restaurant at a certain time on a certain day.

On the appointed day, still a bit skeptical of Kadio's information, I went looking for Stella. I first went to Imus, where she had last lived. In the house where she had lived, I found someone else—who told me that Stella and her family had moved, but she knew not where. I tried for about three hours to find out from someone, anyone, where they were. My efforts availed nothing, so I set out to Las Pinas, hoping that Kadio's word had been true and Stella would meet me there.

The sun had just set when I found the Las Pinas Restaurant. As soon as I parked my car, two hooded Filipino men came out of nowhere and put their guns to my head. They told me to raise my hands, to keep quiet, and to do everything they said. I asked what was going on, and they ignored the question. They just blindfolded me and tied my hands.

I was very frightened, shaking and trembling. They pushed me back into my car, and one of them took the wheel. We drove for about ten minutes and stopped. The three of us transferred to another car and drove for about half an hour. They parked the car, and we walked for maybe ten minutes. We then got into a boat—to my surprise, riding in a boat blindfolded was very difficult, I guess because I could not anticipate and adjust for waves and such. I thought of capsizing the boat and trying to escape—but with my hands bound, that seemed risky. Anyway, the boat ride turned out to be very short, maybe five minutes, so it was over before I could decide to try that route of escape.

After the boat landed, we walked for another half hour or so. We walked through wooded areas, some level but mostly not, sometimes on grass, sometimes on uneven dirt roads with plenty of bumps. I kept stumbling because of the blindfold.

Finally, we stopped. Two or three more men joined my captors, and I could hear them talk in low voices. One of them asked if I already had dinner. That was the first glimmer of hope for me—I did not think they would feed me if they were going to kill me. The guy told me to cooperate with them and my life would be spared. I asked him what this was all about. He said, "The boss will come to talk to you later."

I was still blindfolded, but they told me to grasp something and climb. I realized they were helping me climb up into a bamboo hut. When we got into it, they took off my cloth blindfold, replacing it quickly with a pair of diver's goggles with black-painted lenses. That was another ray of hope—if they wanted me blindfolded, maybe they wanted to make sure I would not recognize anyone after I was released. They tied an electric cord tightly around my waist and bound me to one of the support posts that held up the hut.

They all climbed down out of the hut. I raised my goggles and saw that I was in a kind of hut common on salt and fishpond operations, for the use of the person in charge. The room was about twelve feet square, with a floor made of bamboo strips. The strips were each about an inch-and-a-half wide, with gaps an eighth of an inch between them to let air circulate. The floor joists and the studs for the walls were round bamboo, and the sides and roof were nipa leaves. The door and one swing-out window, made of some kind of coconut leaves, provided cross-ventilation. The whole hut was put together using rattan strips. The stair steps were bamboo. The floor was about four to five feet above ground level. The whole cabin rested on four round bamboo posts, about eight inches in diameter, one at every corner, from the ground up to the roof.

I was so happy when the masked fellow who would turn out to be my regular guard brought my dinner about an hour later. The dinner was really quite good. A pack of Camel cigarettes came with it. I began to be hopeful that I would be released.

My guard, whose name was Pedro, told me that he would give me a light whenever I wanted to smoke. He told me that he had been instructed to let me smoke as much as I wanted, but not to give me the matches.

I was able to sleep for a couple of hours or so. When I woke up at about midnight, the hut was pitch-black—no lantern or any other kind of lighting. I wanted to smoke. Four or five times during the night I woke Pedro for a light. I wanted to smoke more, but I didn't want to waken the guard more than necessary—no need to get him irritated with me.

My stomach hurt from the thick electric wire tied around my waist. I was lying on a mat made of bamboo leaves, laid directly on the hard floor without a mattress. I was used to sleeping on newspaper on bare ground up in the hills with the guerrillas, but the wire really hurt—it twisted tight whenever I lay down. At one point in the night, I complained to my guard, but he said he could not do anything about it until day break.

In the morning, he tried to loosen the wire, but it didn't help much. He asked the man who brought our breakfast to bring something to cushion the wire. That guy later brought an empty sack made of cotton, and that lessened the pain quite a bit. For breakfast, they gave me a plate of fried rice with a whole fried fish, a plate of fresh sliced tomatoes, and a bottle of water. They let me take off the goggles while I ate—they all wore face masks.

As you can imagine, I was preoccupied with figuring out what was going on and my prospects for release. Frankly, I was shocked to be kidnapped—everyone knew I had been a guerrilla who was close to Jim Ferrer, everyone knew my father was a respected leader in the community, and everyone knew of my friendship with Pareng Hiling, who was much feared. My captors had to be very brave or very stupid. Was this some sort of reprisal for guerrilla activities? Was it a simple kidnap-for-ransom? One thing I knew for sure: I had been set up, and when I got free, Kadio, the bakery worker who had given me the false message to meet Stella, would die. My vow not to kill by my own hand must be broken, I thought. As you can imagine, I was livid.

My guard talked all the time. He was really a very boring person, but he loved to jabber. He spoked Tagalog well, but from his accent I knew it was not his first dialect. I surmised that he was originally from another province where they speak a different dialect. I was trying to figure out who my captors were. He was my guard twenty-four hours a day, and he would not tell me why I was being kept captive.

The "Boss," who was supposedly going to tell me what this was all about, did not show up the first day or the second day or the third day or the fourth. My days were mostly eating, smoking, relieving myself, and sleeping. I also did such exercises as I could while bound—stretching, sit-ups, and isometric (muscle tension) exercises under his watchful eye.

My guard would let me read his trashy magazines. All the time, though, my mind was racing with a million things—how this had happened, whether I would be free, whether my family or Pareng Hiling knew I was captive, what they were planning to help me, whether I would ever see Stella again, whether my dreams of America were to end right here. I knew that, if Pareng Hiling knew of my predicament, he would be there in a flash to rescue me, and that my family would surely do whatever could be done for me. But I also knew my absence could have meant nothing to any of them. They all knew I was going on a search for Stella, a search that could lead anywhere and take any amount of time. For all I knew, they were blissfully ignorant of my circumstances.

Most of all, I tried to figure out how to escape. The longer I went without meeting "the Boss," the more concerned I became, and the more seriously I considered taking my freedom into my own hands.

My guard was barely five feet tall, but he was stocky and muscular. He was probably a bit heavier than my 130-140 pounds, though I was about eight inches taller than he. Still, I was not scared of him physically; I was strong and agile. He had a gun, though—a .45 caliber—always tucked into his pants. That was a gun I knew well. During the war, I learned to dismantle and reassemble the gun, to reload it one-handed with either hand, and to use it efficiently. If I could get the gun away from him, I would be in good shape—but if not, well, not so good. The .45 is such a heavy bullet that if you are hit anywhere in your body, the shock to your system will immobilize you immediately.

When and how to escape? I would have to escape during the day, to figure out where I was and get home. Maybe when they took me to the woods each morning to do my bathroom chores? That would be very risky and dangerous—while I did "my business," my guard would stand about ten to fifteen feet away, alert, watching me like a hawk, with his hand on the gun.

Pedro tended to take lots of naps during the day, and since he always snored, I could tell when he was asleep. I decided to try to escape when he was asleep. If I could find a heavy object, I could knock him out and take the gun. (I had already figured out how to get out of the electric cord quickly). But what heavy object could I use? Oh, yes—me! I could jump on his head with my two feet. My whole weight would surely knock him out, I thought. I could then tie him up to the post, take off (with the gun to protect myself), and find my way home—free. I liked that. That was the best idea I had come up with so far. If he woke while I was approaching him, or my jump did not disable him, I would have to move to "Plan B"—wrestle him down, take the gun, and kill him. That was not appealing, but I would do it if necessary.

I began testing how deeply he slept during the day, by making soft noises or slight movements to see how he reacted. You would have thought I was a scientist, so carefully I performed my experiments to see just how long and deeply he slept, what noises would awaken him, how much the hut moved as I moved, and so forth. Unfortunately, the results of the experiments showed that more often than not he would immediately waken and turn his head in my direction at my slightest movement.

As I worked through "Plan A" and "Plan B" in my mind, I decided Plan A was just too risky. The hut was very creaky and shaky—when I jumped, he might waken, roll away, and have the advantage. I decided just to go for a modified Plan B: get free, grab the gun, and shoot him if necessary. I did not plan to kill him; I planned to shoot him in the leg. But I certainly planned to get myself free.

I decided I had to convert him into a deep day-time sleeper—maybe by keeping him up the whole night chain-smoking, asking for a light every few minutes. If I woke him up all night long to let me smoke, maybe he would be worn out the next day.

I only had three cigarettes left, though, so I would have to ask for more and wait until I got them to put my plan into effect.

This was the fourth day, and I was getting restless. I was anxious and uncomfortably filthy—I had not been able to wash or brush my teeth since my capture, and I had been sleeping in my clothes. I feared the onset of one of my malaria attacks—four or five hours of terrible chills, fever, and painful aches. I felt like I was at the point of going crazy, that I could break down any moment. I often felt this edgy, crazy way just before a malaria attack.

I did a lot of deep breathing and kept telling myself to use my head—I knew that acting impulsively would be stupid. I rehearsed my escape plan mentally, over and over, to work out every possible detail.

When my dinner came, to my surprise and delight there were four packs of cigarettes. This would be the night I would instigate my plan! I ate my dinner with great pleasure—shrimps, a whole big female crab, a piece of broiled pork, a bowl of steamed rice, and sauce. I had a mango for dessert.

Below me, several men were talking. My mind was occupied with the plan I had for the evening. The men fell silent, and my guard came to me and said that I would be set free.

I screamed and shouted with joy. My guard said the boss had told him that the ransom money had already been exchanged. I asked him if I could untie myself. He said that it was O.K., but we must do things as ordered. I thought that was just fine, since of course they wanted to protect themselves from punishment for the crime they were committing.

I had eaten all my dinner except for the mango, and I had to go to the bathroom. After I had relieved myself, we headed out. We walked for almost an hour to a boat. The river was just a wide creek, about ten meters wide. The boatman wore a new hat and sunglasses, and across the river were two more men dressed the same. The boatman went across the river to talk with his two companions. About a couple of meters away from me, they had a short conversation, and after a few minutes, they told me that my father and a brother were waiting for me at a designated spot. I was very happy and thankful to Amang and Kaka Mando. I was also thinking about Stella, wondering if she would be with them. Not much chance of that, but I loved the thought of it.

I was told to follow instructions and things would be fine. I told them that I was going to behave like a good altar boy. They laughed at the way I said it.

It was about eight o'clock in the evening and the moon was so low, round and bright. The night was almost like day. I headed out, walking, with one guard. He said his name was Pepe. He was a little taller than my previous guard, but not so stocky. He looked like he had not had enough food during the war but was now regaining his weight. I was thinking that I could lick the guy if we had to fight, any kind of fight—but that I did not have to worry about that anymore, since I was on my way home. I was very joyful, even telling my guide some jokes. Since the moon was full and bright, and I felt so good, I was put in mind of Stella and similar nights we had walked together—and now, I knew, would again. Looking back, I guess it sounds curious to say I was full of romantic images as my guard and I walked the fields. But that's how it was.

Pepe was not talkative like my guard in the hut. He hardly spoke. We were walking on dried rice fields, where the soil was hard, waiting for the rain. The field, like most rice fields, was divided into sections enclosed by dikes. I was not sure how far we were from Paranaque or where my father and brother would be waiting for me. My guide wouldn't even respond to my questions. When we had been walking for about an hour, I could not see any houses for quite a distance, and I began to lose my enthusiasm.

The longer we walked, the less I believed he was taking me to my family. Knowing my father and brother, I was sure they would insist on waiting for me in Paranaque or nearby. I was getting apprehensive and dubious about what was going on.

My hopes and fears were at war. Maybe the kidnappers were just trying to cover their tracks. But maybe they had lied about the ransom, maybe that was not the point at all. The guerrillas had made some enemies, and this could be revenge. My abductors could be lying and making a fool out of me—I could be walking to my own death.

"I've got to use my head and play it cool," I thought to myself. "How can I get free?" I was not blindfolded. My hands were free, except for the mango I had not eaten at dinner, that I had been playing with while we walked.

The guard started holding his .45 pistol in his right hand, instead of tucked into his belt as it had been earlier. He told me to walk ahead, in front of him, and that really bothered me. He began acting nervous and tense. The way he was acting, I was sure that I was not about to be set free.

"I've got to make my move," I thought. "But I've got to do it right. I only get one chance."

I was bigger and stronger than my guard—but he had the gun. I began walking very slowly, with a pronounced (fake) limp, to give myself time to think and maybe get him to let his guard down. I was concentrating on his gun. I could see that the safety lever and the hammer were both down. For him to fire the gun, he had to flick the safety lever up and cock the hammer. If there were no cartridge in the chamber, he also had to pull the slide back and release it quickly—but I could not count on an empty chamber.

Several times, I asked to stop to rest, but I couldn't find the right opportunity to grab the gun. Then I noticed that he was staring at my handmade, white, high-cut leather basketball shoes, which had cost me a bundle. I offered him my shoes, telling him that since I was going home, I could get another pair later. He said, "No thanks," and we kept walking.

During our fifth or sixth stop, he said that maybe he would like to try my shoes on. I hoped that during the shoe exchange, I could kick the gun away from him and wrestle him into submission. No such luck. We took off our shoes and exchanged, but he kept the gun well away from my reach. His shoes were much too small for me, but I had made a deal I couldn't back out of.

We again started to walk, and he started insisting that I walk faster, poking the gun into my back. He pointed toward a house in the distance, perhaps half an hour away, and said my brother and father were waiting there. His nervous tone of voice, though, and his jumpy mannerisms, seemed like he was lying and feared something. I was very angry, ready to explode—I knew, now, I had been misled. My father and brother would not be in that house. I had to make my move.

Each time I paused to go over a dike, I could feel the muzzle of his gun in my back. The last time the gun touched my back, my right foot was on top of the dike. I pivoted hard and hit his right hand—the one holding the gun—with my left hand, following it with a very hard right, with all the power I could muster, straight to his jaw. I prayed the gun would drop and he would fall unconscious, knocked out. It did not come out that way.

He was sort of groggy, but still standing, still holding the gun. I leapt for the gun and grabbed it with both hands, my right hand on the butt and my left on the hammer to keep it from firing. His right hand was on the trigger, and his left hand was free, hitting my face. He was swearing to kill me. He put his left hand on the gun to try to wrestle it away. We were kicking and kneeing each other, biting, elbowing, wrestling, rolling on the ground—it seemed like an hour but may have been only half a minute. My right hand went numb from punching him, but otherwise I was feeling very strong.

I bit his nose and wouldn't let it go, and he blew out snot into my mouth—I swallowed most of it, for I was determined to bite off his nose. Still, I was startled, and he kicked my stomach with his knee. That dazed me, but I was not unconscious. I remember making some big effort—I cannot say exactly what. In a split second, when my mind cleared up, he was lying on his back, about six or seven feet away. I was half seated, almost lying on my back, with my right elbow resting on the ground; I was holding the gun with my left hand.

He jumped up, and I thought he would dive on me. I switched the gun to my right hand, flicked the safety up, and briskly pulled the slide backward. A cartridge jumped out of the ejection port—I was right, the chamber had held a cartridge—but releasing the slide quickly reloaded the chamber. I aimed the gun at him, and he ran, fast, zigzagging and shouting loudly for help from his people. Since he was running so oddly, I could not count on hitting him in the legs, and I remembered my pledge not to kill anyone. Besides, I had nothing personal against him. I jumped up and ran as fast as I could in the opposite direction.

When I had run far enough to be sure no one was following, I slowed to a jog. Even though the moon was still giving plenty of light, I had tripped and fallen a few times, and my knuckles and face hurt from the fight. My feet hurt from running in my guard's too-small shoes. I didn't know where I was. Still, I tucked the gun into my pants and kept jogging.

About an hour later, I think, I saw a small, flickering light in the distance. I continued jogging, aiming for the flickering light. I thought I saw two horses coming up, far behind me. I fired a shot in the air to let them know that I was armed and to make sure the gun worked, in case I needed it. Maybe I scared them off, or maybe I just imagined them, for the riders disappeared.

Finally, I came to a series of low, lighted buildings. Getting closer to the buildings, I found that they were fenced in. I hoped it was a U.S. Army installation, though at night there were no flags flying. I ran around the perimeter of the fence—I could not find the entrance, for it was a huge area. I started crying for help as I ran. When no one answered my cries and I could not find the gate, I climbed the fence. A guard came running.

One of the officers took charge and gave me some water. When I had caught my breath, I told them the whole story. They phoned the Paranaque Police Department—who said they had no idea of the kidnapping, but they knew me and knew I was a good person. I gave a deposition to the U.S. officer, who charged me with trespassing but sent me home with a military driver in a U.S. jeep. As it turns out, the army base was in Alabang, maybe twenty-five miles from my home.

The Paranaque Police had notified my parents that I had set myself free, right after the American officer called. The news apparently spread like wildfire. When I arrived at the Paranaque Municipal Building at about three o'clock in the morning, my family and friends were all there. There were plenty of people, some of them carrying signs. One sign said, "Welcome, Rudy," but the sign that made me most happy said, "Rudy, we have Stella's address." I was so happy that I hugged almost everybody. We all walked home to Don Galo, a fifteen or twenty minute walk.

The first question my mother asked was if I was hungry. I told her that all I needed was a toothbrush and a shower. Once I was cleaned up, I came down to talk.

I wanted to know, first thing, when they had realized that I was missing and how much ransom the kidnappers had demanded.

My father had found the pencil-written ransom note early that very morning—four days after I was abducted. They had not been all that worried about me—after all, I was a big boy, and it wasn't unusual for me to go away for a few days. The note had been in an envelope, tucked through the steel gate of our front walkway—an entrance we did not use regularly. They had been unable to guess when the note had been left, for no one had used that gate for awhile, and the houseboy had not cleaned it in days.

The ransom note demanded one hundred thousand pesos—quite a handsome sum, equal over $50,000 in U.S. dollars today—and said the kidnappers would kill me if the police or other authorities were alerted. It said they wanted the money in small bills and would send instructions for its delivery in seven days. The note, written in a poor hand, was not signed or dated.

Amang and Kaka Mando had been talking and even arguing all day about the situation. Amang insisted that they not tell the police or Pareng Hiling. He had no doubt that the money could be raised within seven days, with the help of my brother, friends, and relatives. However, they did not really know how much time they had left, since they did not know when the note had been left. Kaka Mando later told me that he had tried to talk Amang into telling the police or Jim Ferrer—who was the most powerful man in Paranaque in those days. Amang was unfazed. They would comply fully with the kidnappers' demands—that was his order.

Amang and Kaka Mando, with a few trusted friends and relatives, were in a closed-door meeting, figuring out how to raise the money, when the police broke the good news that I was free. So the planning changed to how to celebrate instead of coming up with the ransom.

All the time we were talking, neighbors and relatives kept coming, bringing food, up until sunrise, when I excused myself to go to bed. That was a Sunday, so for most people it was a "no work" day. When I woke up at eleven in the morning, the party was still going on. After lunch I went to bed again. When I woke up at seven in the evening, most people were gone, except for a few close relatives cleaning our place.

The next morning, after a long shower, a good breakfast, a haircut, and a shave, I went to see Stella. She and her family had just moved to San Dionisio, another barrio of Paranaque, only a few miles from Don Galo.

Stella was surprised and elated when I appeared at her steps. She had known that I was missing, for as soon as my family found the ransom note, they had scoured Don Galo to discover where Stella lived, then sent someone to see whether she had any clue to my whereabouts. In the middle of the night, when I was freed, no one had thought to go tell her! We had a very joyous reunion. We talked for hours, as I told her every detail and many other things I had never shared (like the story I shall tell you in the next chapter), until I had to go home. We parted very happy to be together, and I promised to see her again soon.

I became sort of a local hero. The police assigned two bodyguards to stay with me all the time, and I started carrying a semiautomatic hand gun, a German Luger P-38, for self-protection. Wherever I went, my two police guards were nearby. Everybody knew my tale, and people kept asking questions about it. (Like, "So did you manage to bite off that guy's nose?" No—but the memory of swallowing his snot kept grossing me out, as it does even today.) I lost all my privacy. I did not like it at all.

Within a month Kadio (the bakery helper), Pedro (my guard), and Pepe (the guide that last night) were all apprehended and indicted, along with a couple of John Does. One of the gang turned state's evidence, and the John Does were soon apprehended. The kidnappers, it turned out, were a gang of criminals from a faraway town, who traveled the country kidnapping people. They had brutally murdered several victims whose families had failed to meet the demands.

The kidnappers could not post bond, for their bails were set very high. That was fine with me—I was able to get rid of my bodyguards. Without them, I felt so free.

That freedom was short-lived. Within a few weeks, I was in jail myself. Before long, I would be the plaintiff in one trial and the accused in another.

Chapter Six

Charged with Murder

The end of the war should have started a great time for me—young, proud, free, and in love. I was a bit of a local hero, known for my courage in escaping my kidnappers. But the worst was yet to come.

We guerrillas had not been paid for military service during the war. With the liberation of our country, the Philippines Veterans Board (P.V.B.) was set up to provide back pay. Hundreds of thousands of people suddenly appeared claiming to have been guerrillas. Fortunately for me, Jim Ferrer ran the P.V.B., so there was never any question about my claim. I quickly received back pay—not very much, since I was considered a buck private, but enough to make the point that I had truly served. I bought a 1936 Indian motorcycle with some of my pay.

I had decided to start college in the Fall of 1946, so in the Spring, after we had pretty well recovered from the ravages of war, when I was flush with the joy of escaping my kidnappers, I had plenty of time for playing basketball, gambling, seeing Stella, and being with my friends.

So far, so good. Stella's health started failing, once again, though. The doctors wanted her to move north to Baguio, where they thought the cool climate would help her.

Baguio was a beautiful place, a resort town built by the American colonialists to resemble the resorts of New England or the Catskills. It was a couple of hundred miles from Don Galo, though, and the roads were very bad. Stella and I did not know how we would see each other. We did not know whether she would recover enough to resume our life and our plans for the future. As she left for Baguio, we were very unhappy. We held each other so tenderly and wept as she prepared to go. Our future was so uncertain, and we were heartbroken.

For good or ill, she could not stand the cold weather in Baguio, even if the doctors wanted her there. She did not want to be so far from me, either. Within a month, she came back to Paranaque. I was overjoyed.

But then came my arrest.

One afternoon, I was in a friend's garage working on my motorcycle, which needed an engine overhaul and a new paint job. Two well-dressed Filipinos approached me and asked if I were Rudy de Lara. I said, "Of course," and they identified themselves as agents of the National Bureau of Investigation, or N.B.I., which was the F.B.I. of the Philippines. They displayed their badges and presented a warrant for my arrest.

One of them cuffed my hands behind my back and told me to remain silent. I was terrified, not knowing what it was all about or what the consequences might be. It reminded me of the kidnapping, when two men had come from nowhere and put their guns to my head. This time, though, these men were very polite and extremely nice, if you can say that about someone who is arresting you.

It was a very warm day in March, in the heart of the dry season. I had no shirt on; I was wearing only sports shorts. The N.B.I. men began walking me to their car, about four blocks away, near my home, and explained to me why I was under arrest. Our neighbors began gathering, wondering what I had done to be shackled—especially since only for serious offenses would you be cuffed behind your back. Only so very recently those neighbors had called me a hero for freeing myself from my kidnappers, and now I was being humiliated for something, they knew not what, that must have been very bad. By the time we had made it to the car, quite a crowd had gathered.

As I was pushed into the car, my father came out of the house, with my mother beside him, crying. "Why, why, why," they screamed, as the car started moving slowly through the crowd. I shouted back, through the slightly opened window, that it was about the disappearance of Dr. Gabriel.

The car moved away slowly through the crowd. One of our household helpers caught up alongside and handed me a warm-up suit to cover myself. I shouted back that I needed some light clothing. The N.B.I. agents seemed concerned about all the people—one of them said, "You're a popular man." Nevertheless, the crowd was curious, not confrontational, and the car got free and headed toward prison.

Now I must tell you about the disappearance of Dr. Juan—the mayor of Paranaque, in whose compound I had helped butcher the pig, where the bombshell had killed the little boy, just after we liberated Don Galo.

This is the secret mission to Imus that I had gotten myself involved in, more than a year before, in February, 1945, so that I could see Stella.

You remember that I had been forbidden to go on the mission, despite my efforts to be included. When I had finally gotten permission, I ran home to tell my father that I would be able to see Stella. Amang questioned the wisdom of the trip, since I did not know the mission, and since there were still many Japanese soldiers on the loose. I told him not to worry about it. I was a triumphant guerrilla, with a chance to see my girl. What more did I need to know?

We left for Imus shortly after sundown. Seven of us headed out in two cars. I was told to take the shorter of the two main routes from Don Galo to Imus, through the town of Bacoor. As we approached Bacoor, we heard the sounds of a gun battle, and when we reached the town, we discovered that the bridge linking Bacoor and Imus had blown up a short while earlier—our guerrilla compatriots in Bacoor told us that the Japanese soldiers had left the night before, that some lingered in the area, and that they had apparently planted a timebomb on the bridge as they left. Now we had to take the longer route to Imus, through territory full of Japs. We were lightly armed, with handguns and two semi-automatic carbines. Our leader decided we should not risk a night-time gunfight, so we would stay overnight in Bacoor.

The Bacoor guerrillas fed us dinner and put us in a school building to sleep. Sleep eluded me, though. I was preoccupied with three things: the Jap-infested territory we would go through the next day (especially with the sounds of the gun battle in my head), Stella, and a huge boil on my backside. You might think I shouldn't mention a boil on my butt, but life is not always polite or romantic. No, a boil is not heroic or adventurous, and dealing with it has nothing to do with courage, but pain has a way of demanding your attention no matter what else is going on. Remember that at this point, I had been in the fields with the guerrillas for several weeks, and neither food nor hygiene had been the best. I had never had such a painful boil before.

Very early in the morning, around three or four o'clock, we had breakfast and headed out. The sun was about to rise when we arrived in Imus. The other six guerrillas got out—they told me to stay with the cars. They all walked a block farther in great haste. As soon as they were out of sight, I asked the first person I saw if she knew where Stella's family was staying. They were staying in the house right in front of me!

Although it was quite early in the morning for a visit, Stella and her mother came down when I knocked and called out. They were, of course, quite surprised—and as I have already said, I was shocked to see how thin and sick Stella had become. I told them I was there with the guerrillas on a mission—by this time, guerrillas did not have to keep our identities secret and couldn't have, anyway, since we had been attached to the U.S. forces. While I struggled with my emotions—happiness to see her, terror at her condition—we started catching up on news of everyone we all knew. After only five minutes or so my group leader shouted, "Rudy, we have to go."

I had no wish to go—with her mother present, we had hardly gotten through the rudimentary parts of our conversation, and I needed to know more about her condition. I answered back that they had to wait a few minutes. He almost exploded, shouting back emphatically, "We've got to go right now, dammit!" Clearly, my needs and wishes were irrelevant to his agenda, so like a good soldier, I went back to my car as ordered. I was shocked to see Dr. Juan Gabriel, the mayor of Paranaque, in the passenger seat, with two guerrillas in the back. I was puzzled and speechless. Dr. Juan looked pale and frightened but greeted me, softly, with, "Hello Rudy."

I had known Dr. Juan very well since my childhood. He was a medical doctor, who had treated me many times, in his office and at my home. He was my father's friend, and my mother played cards with his wife almost every day. He was also godfather to my younger brother, Tommy, so he was a member of our family. He was kind and a very caring person. He was a very popular mayor, both before and during the war, and so far as I knew, a good one. My father and Dr. Juan were not in the same political party, but my father had voted for him.

The leader of our group told me to take the lead and head back to Paranaque—he and the others would follow. As we drove away, Dr. Juan's wife, Ka Tanging, ran to my car window and whispered to me, "You take care of him, OK, Rudy?" I told her, "Yes, Mom, don't worry, I will try my best."

The atmosphere in the car was tense and silent. No one would tell me what was up—which insulted and angered me. I was working my brain overtime, wondering what we were up to. My head was full of questions with no sensible answers.

It took us about an hour and a half to drive to Paranaque. The road was bad with plenty of pot holes and bomb craters. When we entered Paranaque, the other car passed me and led us to the main headquarters of the ROTC Hunters, a hastily-installed, portable building located just past Las Pinas, in what was then called Wakas. My compatriots all got out of the cars. The other car left, and I was told to stay put with the mayor.

When they were all gone, and it was only the mayor and me in the car, his first words were, "Why do they want me in Paranaque?" I told the mayor that I really did not know—and that was the truth, so help me, God. He was worried and really opened up. He told me all about his concerns and doubts. He poured out everything on his mind, talking to me like a father to a son. I told him all about my parents, brothers, and sisters. Honestly, I remember the tone of the conversation—the intimacy—more than I remember the words. But that tone was very touching, as this man I admired, adored, and respected treated me like a trusted son.

He noticed from the way I was sitting and squirming and wincing that I was in pain, and he asked why. I told him about my boil. He said that he wanted to look at it. I hesitated—it hardly seemed like an important matter, under the circumstances—but he insisted. I showed it to him. He said it was already oozing and asked me if I wanted him to work on it—but before I could consent, he gave an expert squeeze and lanced the boil by hand. He used his own handkerchief to clean me up. The pain subsided almost instantly. That was quite a relief, and I thanked him over and over.

We went back to chatting. He told me, among other things, about the house he had rented next to the one Stella's parents had rented. He was looking after Stella, and he explained to me the details of her precarious health. That part of the conversation, I will never forget.

Eventually, we ran out of things to say, and—free from the pain that had been bothering me for days—I fell asleep. I woke up when my leader came out of headquarters. Dr. Juan was still seated beside me. It was almost noon. The guerrilla leader asked politely that Dr. Juan follow him inside the headquarters, and he told me I could go home.

I was thinking while driving home that there was something very strange about my participation and the way I was treated. Why had I been kept in the dark about the mission? I couldn't figure why they couldn't give me more time with Stella, nor why I had been left with Dr. Juan, alone in the car, for a couple of hours. In reality, I had been ordered around like a slave, not treated like a veteran guerrilla. None of it made much sense to me.

When I got home, and after eating a little, I told my father about the secret mission, including the makeshift "surgery" his compadre had performed on me. Amang boiled some water with guava leaves and plenty of salt and cleaned my boil, then pounded the leaves and salt into a paste (his favorite cure for skin problems), and applied the paste to my backside. Feeling better but still tired for lack of sleep, I went to bed.

I had not been sleeping very long when my father woke me up to say that word in the street had it that Dr. Juan had been shot. No one knew why, when, or where, he said, but the town was abuzz with the rumor.

Oh, my God! I was terrified that I now understood the mission, and that I knew pretty much where and when he had been killed—sometime during the last four hours, in Wakas. Anger and fear welled up in me. "I could be accused of this," I told my father.

I went looking for an explanation—I was so livid and sad. I met with one of the guerrilla leaders. He told me that Dr. Juan had been a Japanese collaborator, tried, convicted, and sentenced to death by the guerrillas. He said the reason I had been forbidden to go on the trip, then treated so brusquely and kept in the dark, was that they knew Dr. Juan was my godfather (I corrected him that he was Tommy's godfather), and they feared I would do something to help him escape if they knew what we were up to.

I do not have the words to describe my mental state. Yes, they were right—if I had known what they were up to, I probably would have helped Dr. Juan escape. And how well they had deceived me—even Dr. Juan had not realized he was about to die, or he surely would have escaped when I was asleep in the car. And the assurances I had given his wife! I was angry, ashamed, sad, and humiliated—outraged.

I personally did not believe that all cooperation with the Japanese amounted to treason and deserved death. While many public officials openly collaborated with the Japanese—and were assassinated by both Filipino and American guerrillas—to my knowledge, Dr. Juan was not one of them. The worst thing that he had probably done was to follow orders from the occupying forces, like demanding local salt producers to supply the Japanese army. According to my father, the Japs paid them the going market prices. Yes, the mayor forced our people to supply the Japanese, but what choice did he have? In any case, I did not believe he should have been tried, convicted, sentenced, and executed in a private guerrilla court, without a chance to defend himself.

The way I saw it, the execution of Dr. Juan was part of a bigger problem. After years of secrecy and fear, some guerrillas were getting out of control, now that they could operate freely. I knew quite well of some heinous acts by the guerrillas—Rufing Balinghasay, the husband of my cousin Carling Balinghasay, the only daughter of my mother's sister, was brutally shot dead in the presence of his four young children. Kaka Rufing had simply refused to give his truck to a guerrilla, who only wanted it for his own pleasure. The killing of Kaka Rufing was only one of many cases I knew about. For me, the killing of Dr. Juan was the last straw.

I went to our local ROTC Hunters headquarters and submitted my resignation—which was accepted a week later by our barrio commander, Captain Romy de Jesus.

The day my resignation was to be finalized, I went to the headquarters. At one point, I went out to the latrine, where I smelled a foul odor, like a dead dog. I started to light a cigarette but could not stand the obnoxious odor. I went inside without even doing my business, to tell the guy who ran the office about the odor. He took me by the arm and told me that Dr. Juan was buried in a shallow grave next to the toilet. All my hair stood up. I shivered all over and felt so sick to my stomach. I had to step out in front of the quarters to vomit.

The thought of Dr. Juan's rotting body, right beside the outhouse, wracked my system, triggering a malaria attack. I went straight home, vomiting more and more the whole way, my head beginning to ache and my body shaking with chills. My father covered me with blankets, and eventually I slept.

I never went to guerrilla headquarters again. I am proud to have served my country, but I was done with the guerrillas.

At least, I thought I was done with the guerrillas. I was wrong. Now, a year later, the morning papers had the headline: "The Disappearance of Dr. Gabriel, Mayor of Paranaque, Solved. Seven Men under Arrest. A John Doe Involved." The seven accused men included Mike Bernabe, Leonardo Caneda, Nicanor Ison, Dwight Velasco, Pareng Tangol, Piping Pangat, and me. (I am not sure I remember the exact full names of the accused after all these years.) I think the "John Doe" was supposed to be whatever senior ROTC Hunter official gave the order for the execution, but they lacked the evidence to specify who that was. Nearly everyone suspected it was Jim Ferrer, but I rather doubted that, by now. I had decided this was a renegade action by guerrillas out of control.

The Gabriel family was one of the wealthiest in the Philippines—as it still is. Mrs. Tanging Gabriel, the widow of the mayor, was determined to have justice, or else Dr. Juan's death would probably have disappeared as just another act of war. Instead, the papers covered the story repeatedly for over a year. Dr. Juan's death became part of local lore—even today, when I visit the Philippines I am sometimes asked about it.

The seven of us were detained in four different prisons. I was sent to the Bilibid Prison in Manila, together with Leonardo Caneda, whom I called my Pareng Nardo. This was the prison for hopelessly hardcore criminals. We were placed in Cell No. 2 with criminals accused of murder, rape, and kidnapping.

In the Philippine prisons at that time, each cell was run by a prisoner, sort of like the "trusty" system in the U.S., but with more power. The cell captain really ran things inside the cell. The cell captain of Cell No. 2 was frightening just to look at. He was huge, about six feet, four inches tall, 250 pounds, with tattoos all over his body, and big eyes that looked evil set into a heavily-scarred face. He looked like he would kill you if you just said something wrong. This was the first time in my life I had been scared simply of someone's presence.

Our fellow prisoners greeted us like brothers, in a sense—after all, they liked the idea that we were murderers. Many of them were well-known criminals we had read about in the papers. So far as they were concerned, though, we were their equals, murderers. That was actually nice.

That was the only thing nice about Cell No. 2. Early in our stay, the cell captain asked us if we knew the guerrillas in Paranaque. We told him that in fact we were guerrillas—after all, it was hardly a secret, since that's why we were in prison. Besides, we were proud: the war was over and we had won. He reacted with a frightening smile and started asking questions in a hateful tone of voice. I suddenly knew we had made a mistake, admitting we had been guerrillas.

He did not like our answers to his questions—a friend of his had been killed, perhaps by guerrillas from Paranaque—and he started torturing us, one at a time. We were slapped in the face and punched, at first all over but then only in the stomach, over and over and over. He and his cronies took turns questioning us, questioning me while Pareng Nardo was waiting for his turn and vice-versa. We had to watch each other's suffering, knowing we were next. They kept saying that their friend had been killed by the guerrillas and we knew something about it. In truth, we had no idea who or what they were talking about, but every denial got us a punch in the stomach.

We were under the third-degree for over two weeks. During the daytime, we had to work, cleaning the prison, on our hands and knees with rags—mops and brooms were not allowed, lest we use them as weapons. Adding insult to injury, we also had to give our tormentors full-body massages. Then at night we were tortured. The torturers seemed to get big kicks out of it. It was very humiliating. At one point, I almost fought back, but I stifled that dangerous urge.

Those men were vicious. They punched our stomachs, just around the belly button, so hard and so often that they virtually crippled us. It hurt so much that I could not even eat or sleep. Lying down on the army cot wracked me with pain, and getting up in the morning was almost impossible.

This went on until I was visited by my family, who brought with them my friends Pareng Hiling and Paquito Lapid. They were inside the prison compound, but outside the ten-foot fence surrounding the three cells that reputedly housed the most dangerous criminals in the Philippines. I barely made it to the fence to see them, walking in agony, with my body bent like an old man's. My stomach hurt so much that I could hardly stand up. They were shocked to see me like that. My mother started crying, sobbing loudly.

They went to see the prison authorities, and Pareng Nardo and I were immediately transferred to Cell No. 3.

There was a world of difference between the two cells. The cell captain in cell No. 3, named Pat, was from the town of Pateros in the same province as Paranaque. He was also a guerrilla, about twice my age. He was in prison for killing more than sixty people in a matter of days, because he went crazy toward the end of the war. He had just snapped, thinking everyone was a Jap out to get him.

By the time we knew him, he had recovered his mental stability. He liked us and took us under his wing. I talked to Pat for hours and hours—I enjoyed listening to him. He was very intelligent, witty, funny, and told interesting stories. He had participated in attacking a Japanese barracks, killing hundreds, during the war. As cell captain, he was truly in charge. He announced to everyone that he did not want anybody bothering us. Whenever I thought about the cell captain in cell No. 2, the more I liked Pat. Pareng Nardo and I could now sleep soundly, recuperating from the battered stomachs.

All during our imprisonment, our daily ration was canned salmon and steamed rice, three times a day—with some vegetables thrown in at dinner. I enjoyed that at first, but soon I could not stand it. The whole cell stank of salmon—which I do not like anymore, to this day.

My parents arranged to begin sending me food, since Bilibad Prison was only about ten miles from Don Galo. I always shared my food with others, specially with my new friend and protector, Pat. Pareng Nardo's wife also prepared food and had it brought with mine by our driver.

Without the cruelty of Cell No. 2, and with good food, prison life was not as bad as before. Still, we felt very bad. Our lawyers were having trouble arranging the setting of bail, and we did not know when we would be freed on bond. And life inside was still no picnic. We had neither fans nor air conditioning, and hygiene was rudimentary. For instance, there was one water spigot per cell, and we had to take turns washing ourselves, naked, in front of everyone. And violence was still a reality—our roommates, after all, were not choir boys.

One night, as soon as the lights were turned out at midnight, six inmates in our cell got into a fight. I yelled for Pat to break it up. He yelled back, "Let them kill each other." They had knives made from the handles of the army mess kits that we had been using as plates. All of them ended up in the hospital; two died. The others returned to the cell a week or so later. After that, lights were left on all night.

We were allowed to receive visitors once a week or meet with our lawyers daily. As I recall, our lawyer only came once, but our families and friends came faithfully, every week. Stella and I wrote notes to each other. Right after I was imprisoned, she asked if she could come visit me, but I refused. I did not want her in the dirty prison, out in the heat—but most of all, I did not want her seeing me like this, caged with the worst criminals in the Philippines. I also told my father not to allow Inang or Kaka Cely or any other women to come for visits, after that first one. The visits from my father and brothers and friends, and constant letters from Stella, kept me going, hoping for better things to come.

I had been in prison a bit over three months when the word came that an arraignment and bail hearing had finally been set.

On the day of the hearing, I was shackled with both hands behind my back and deposited into the back seat of a U.S. Army surplus jeep, with a guard beside me and another one driving. I complained that my shackled hands hurt, since I had to lean back on them, and I asked if I could be cuffed with my hands in front of me. The guard beside me said that was against the law, but since I didn't look like a hardened criminal, he would cuff me to him, my right hand to his left. I thanked him, for that was much better.

The ride from the Bilibid Prison to Paranaque, about a ten mile ride, was exciting. We took an extremely round-about route, which perplexed me—I learned later that there had been rumors that our former guerrilla *compadres* intended to break us free along the way. Some of the sites we passed were very sad—destruction from the war—but mostly I was excited to see how rapidly Manila was rebuilding, just in the time I had been in prison. One site for which Manila would become famous had just begun to appear—"jeepneys," brightly decorated Army surplus jeeps used as taxis and general-purpose conveyances.

As we approached the Paranaque Municipal Building, I saw a huge crowd of people. We entered the parking lot with difficulty, weaving our way through the crowd—mostly friends and families of the accused. I recognized almost everyone. Some waved signs, and I waved back. I was so elated to see such support from my family and friends. The only sadness about that part was that Stella was not in the crowd—the arraignment had been set at a time when she and her family were away.

The two-story municipal building was small. There were two cells on the ground floor. They put me in one, waiting for the other defendants we were shipped separately, like hard-core criminals. In due course, four of us occupied one cell and three occupied another. The arraignment was sort of a reunion for the seven of us. I was always with Pareng Nardo in prison, but I had not seen the other five since we abducted the mayor.

We were brought upstairs soon after our lawyers arrived. Dr. Gabriel's wife had engaged the services of Senator Vicente Francisco, a famous, powerful litigator, as the lead prosecutor, assisted by some of the most able lawyers in the Philippines. For the defense, Jim Ferrer—who had already been a lawyer before the war—was in charge behind the scenes, with the famous defense lawyer, Senator Quintin Paredes, heading the team of litigators. Ferdinand Marcos was not yet part of the team—I met him the next year, shortly before the trial itself began.

The arraignment lasted the whole morning, and it was something of a circus. When our lawyers had the floor, they spoke in Spanish and English. When the prosecutors had the floor, they spoke in English and Tagalog. The lawyers had quite an argument about what language to use. The judge ruled that the three languages were all acceptable. We entered our plea of "Not guilty" in English.

The prosecutor argued that we should not be released on bail, since we were dangerous and, as experienced guerrillas, could easily skip bail and hide in the mountains. I thought that guy had no clue—all I wanted to do was go home.

The judge denied the prosecutor's motion and set bail at one million pesos—something like half a million dollars in today's U.S. currency—per person. The prosecutor argued that the amount was too low and should be doubled. Our lawyer argued that the amount was excessive and should be reduced by half, since raising a total of seven million pesos would be extremely difficult. The judge was unfazed; bail remained at one million pesos each.

To my consternation, we were carted back to jail. Our supporters did not have the money for that kind of bail. I was very unhappy, for long before the hearing, we had been assured by our lawyers that with the number of supporters we had, we could meet any amount the judge would set. That was just hot air.

My father told me that the people responsible for our defense were really working very hard to come up with the bail bond. We had plenty of wealthy backers, but still, the amount of money to be raised for the interest to the bondsmen alone was quite handsome.

Within a couple of weeks, though, the bond was raised, and we were set free. I joked with Pareng Nardo that, as a defendant, I was worth ten times as much as I had been as a kidnap victim, when the ransom demand had been 100,000 pesos.

We had spent about four months in prison.

While I was in prison, the trial of my kidnappers was supposed to get underway. Needless to say, my imprisonment did not speed things up. Then, when I was bailed out, my involvement in the trial of my kidnappers—and my hearing on the trespassing charge at the U.S. Army Base, at which the charges were dropped—slowed down my murder trial. Back and forth, from one courtroom to another—I felt like a professional trial participant.

In the case of the kidnappers, the trial itself is not really much of a story. The story is the corruption of the process—which, as I have said many times, was not unusual in the Philippines—and how we finally resolved it.

The kidnappers' lawyers engaged in witness tampering and bribery, with no respect for the law. High-powered politicians with connections to the defendants approached my father, asking him to forgive the kidnappers and drop the charges. They were not able to make him agree, and they turned to me with the same plea. They thought I could be intimidated, but I was unfazed, and I turned them down. This group of criminals were heinous, wicked, hateful men. I could not forgive them.

The "fixers" kept coming back and back and back, and they finally approached my very-religious mother. My mother begged me to be responsive to them and to forgive. She was adamant about it. She quoted the words "To err is human, to forgive divine," but she said them in our native language, Tagalog, which made the words more meaningful and powerful to me. This was my mother asking me to forgive. How could I say no, to a woman I loved? She suggested that we demand certain conditions that might free our town of all kidnapping, a crime rampant after the war. That sounded very good to me.

She sent a message to the fixers to come to our house and bring all the defendants. In short, my mother told them that I would forgive the defendants if and only if they became accountable for any future kidnappings in our province. If there were any more kidnappings at all, we would come after them tooth-and-nail. The defendants agreed. I added that the necklace they had taken from me, with Stella's photo inside the locket, be returned. They agreed to that, too. I did not know at the time how important that would turn out to be—that in just a little while, Stella would be gone, and I would never again have the chance for another picture.

We all signed a piece of paper spelling out our agreement. The criminal suit against the defendants was dropped. In our province, kidnapping for ransom suddenly ended.

With all the complications and the legal maneuvering, my trial for murder would not get underway for nearly another year after I got out of prison. Before that, I had something far worse to face.

Chapter Seven

When Stella Died

In the Philippines, we have a saying, "*Bahala na,*" which means, "What will be, will be." To American ears, that sounds preposterous, like the thing psychologists call "denial," perhaps. But it describes a basic part of our way of thinking. Once I was bailed out, my attitude toward the impending trial was, in part, "*Bahala na.*" I had things to do, to get on with my life. So I did.

Stella was living now in San Dionisio, a barrio of Paranaque. Her health had once again rebounded, and she seemed fine. She could play piano all she wanted, and we could do most anything we pleased. For a couple of months, I would regularly ride my motorcycle to see her—but being the reserved sort, she would never ride it with me! In the rainy season, though,

I got tired of the motorcycle—riding in the rain is no fun, especially when the temperature is hot and the air is steamy—and sold it for a handsome profit. My Hudson pickup truck, fruits of war, was now in good running condition, after I poured a lot of work into it. Stella and I went out all the time—to restaurants, to movies in Manila, to the beach, and so forth. She would come to Don Galo to see me in my home. She had two close relatives in Don Galo, and she would stay with them for a day or two so we could visit our old haunts.

She asked me once to take her to Mandaluyong, to see the relatives with whom she had stayed during part of the war. She wanted to show them a healthy and stunningly beautiful Stella. That was a wonderful trip—I had seldom seen her happier. On our way home from Mandaluyong, she wanted me to show her the building where I was detained by the Japanese after my last trip to Mandaluyong, during the war. She wanted to see the building because she had spent a few sleepless nights worrying about me even after she found my wallet in Mandaluyong. We found only the skeleton of the building—it had been destroyed during the retreat of the defeated occupiers.

I remember that whenever we went out, I always bought her "*kampuput*" lei, which were sold everywhere in the streets for very little money. A *kampuput* lei is a string of *sampaguita* and *ilang-ilang* flowers that women wear like necklaces. Three *ilang-ilang* flowers hang at the center—each flower has seven long greenish-yellow petals about inch and a half in length—and about eight *sampaguita* flowers are strung on each side. A *sampaguita* flower is about half an inch in diameter and looks like a small white rose. Each flower sends out a lovely, distinct fragrance, and together, the combined fragrance is out of this world. Stella loved the sweet fragrance and always hung the lei near her bed.

I had enrolled in Far Eastern University to get a strong academic record, so we could go to America. We had decided that we would marry after I finished F.E.U. and go to America together. Going to America together filled our dreams. Since my strongest subject was mathematics, and the most practical subject for someone with that kind of talent was engineering, I had decided to study engineering. I cannot say I had any great interest in it for its own sake. That just seemed like the best way to get to America.

Not too long after I got out of prison, the Philippines received its independence, on July 4, 1946. Stella and I spent the afternoon together, but for the evening I had a favor to discharge. A distant cousin and favorite dancing partner of mine had become the "number two wife" of a prominent politician. (Because of the Spaniards, our Catholic country did not allow divorce, so many men had more than one wife and family.) This politician had to take his "number one wife" to all the official festivities. My cousin wanted to make him jealous by showing up on the arm of a handsome young man. I was only too happy to oblige. Stella's jealousy rose up, but I convinced her I really owed this cousin a favor; so she agreed.

By the Fall, I was quite busy with school, playing basketball, and spending time with Stella. In the late Fall, I had a little break from school, and my very good friend, Paquito Lapid, invited me to spend a week in his home town in Pampanga. When I came home from Pampanga, I found my mother sobbing. I asked what was wrong.

"Oh, Rudy, it's Stella," she cried. I was confused. Only a few days before, an x-ray had shown her lungs to be clear, and she had seemed perfectly healthy—we had been out and about, as always. But my mother was in such anguish, so broken-hearted, that I thought Stella must be dead. "No, no," Amang, said, "But it is very bad."

Stella had suffered a stroke. Her blood pressure had soared, and her liver seemed to have been harmed some way, perhaps from medication. She was in and out of a coma. She was under the care of her uncle, since most hospitals had been destroyed in the war, and those that had been rebuilt were still only equipped to handle basic emergencies. Her parents had called the Catholic priest to pray for her in her house—not the last rites; it was merely Filipino custom to call in the priest for dire cases. Her friends and relatives had been with her. Most of the time she was sleeping or unconscious. Whenever she was conscious, she had been asking for me.

I just took a quick shower and a shave and went to see her. She was either sleeping or in a coma when I got to her house. Her mother cried when she saw me. We were talking in low voices in Stella's room when her mother noticed that Stella had opened her eyes. In a whisper Stella asked, "Was that Rudy talking?" Her mother looked at me and left the room.

"Yes, Stella, it's me," I said. She looked as if nothing were wrong with her, as if she were just waking from a lovely nap. She was very happy, smiling, with her eyes glowing. She asked me to help her sit up, and I did.

Her sense of humor was still lively, and we had a wonderful talk. She kept saying, "I'm so happy to see you. I love you. Please don't ever leave me." Her voice was soft but strong and she listened attentively to everything I was saying. Then she closed her eyes and appeared to fall asleep, still with a faint smile on her face.

I stopped talking. I stayed beside her, waiting for her to wake up. She looked like she was sleeping, but I could not tell the difference between sleep and a coma. I tiptoed to the living room and asked her mother if Stella was O.K. She said that Stella was just sleeping and, as always, would wake up any moment. I waited another hour or so, then I excused myself. I said that I would be back after awhile, to be with her when she woke up.

I went home and sat down to supper. Before I finished, a messenger came to tell us that Stella had just passed away. I was shocked. I was devastated. Thinking of what Stella had implored of me just a few hours ago, I wished I had not left. I was ravaged with sorrow and guilt.

I could never have imagined the horrible pain I felt. I thought it was the end of me, the end of every dream—for truly, every dream that defined my hopes and plans had Stella at the center. Nothing I had ever been through had felt nearly so crushing. Even the initial news of her illness, which had torn me apart, did not compare.

I almost did not want to see her dead, not breathing, but I went back to her house anyway. When her mother and her grandmother saw me enter, they wept for me. They knew that Stella and I had dreamed of going to America, a married couple with a new life in a new world. They knew what this death was doing to me, and they felt compassion.

Everyone was very good to me during this time—my family was with me much of the time. In the Philippines, it is customary for loved ones to stay with the dead person all the time until interment, and I stayed with Stella. I did not go to school or give any attention to other things I had to do, not even legal things having to do with my upcoming trial. Except for helping the family plan the funeral and driving them around to make the arrangements, I was inseparable from Stella after her death.

At the funeral, there were eight pallbearers. We carried her from her house, where she had been lying in wake, to the church, then from the church to the place of interment. According to our custom, a band walked ahead of a funeral procession playing music. As we left the church, contrary to custom, they began playing the sad, soft music of Franz Schubert's *Serenade*.

We gathered around her final resting place. I was next to her when the band that had played all during the procession finally stopped. After we bade Stella goodbye, as we waited for the final act of interment, a violin soloist started playing—hardly audible at first, and then a little louder, a very slow, sad, soft, soothing, penetrating violin solo: Stella's own interpretation of Schubert's *Serenade*, yet again. I could not bear it; I could not stop the flow of my tears. I told a friend to stop the music. This theme of private joy should not be played in this time of public sorrow. My efforts were to no avail; my friend knew that I spoke in anguish, not wisdom. So I turned and walked away from the grave, slowly, almost stumbling, like a man in a trance, far enough away to soften the effect of the sweet and penetrating music. I went far, very far. I could not help but weep uncontrollably, without shame, as if I would never stop.

Her mother confided to me later that Stella had insisted to her that, if the end should come, she wanted our song to be played.

Over half a century later, hearing our music reminds me of the good and happy moments we had, but at the same time makes me feel sad. Even today, I sometimes cannot help but weep. The *Serenade* became for me a music of serene sadness.

After the funeral, we observed the customary nine days of prayer at her home, followed by "*sara*," a celebration of sorts that closes out the time of prayer, on the tenth night. I was there every single night. Formally, a full year of mourning followed Stella's death. Her mother and grandmother wore black dresses, while the stepfather had a black ribbon wrapped around his left arm. I wore a small black ribbon, an inch wide, pinned into my left shirt breast pocket, with the top inch showing. The mourning officially ended after one year, but mine lasted very much longer, as we shall see.

Shortly after her passing, and a few times later, I saw an apparition of Stella, in a long white dress. I told my parents and a friend. They all believed I had really seen her ghost, Stella in the form of an angel. I never believed that literally; even then, I thought that was the work of my imagination, driven by my deep wish to have her back. My wish was even deeper than I knew, as I would find out only years later.

Chapter Eight

On Trial

I must tell you about the murder trial, though in truth, I hardly cared about it or paid attention to it. I was mostly trying to cope with Stella's death, throwing myself into my studies. I would come to court and bury myself in my books for the most part, or pay attention to trivial details, like the clothes and mannerisms of the various attorneys. *Bahala na.*

The trial was held in a large room, filled with family members and journalists. We had no jury; the judge would decide our fate. By the time the trial started, not only the seven who had been arrested but three John Does were included. I thought then, as I continue to think, that the prosecutor was really after Jim Ferrer and Terry Adevoso (the founder of the ROTC Hunters), and maybe Sixto Clemente, but lacked the evidence to name them.

The prosecutor, an elderly man, overweight, wearing a well-worn suit, opened the proceedings. I remember that he said this was a case of the Republic of the Philippines against the seven defendants and three John Does. I remember thinking that was not really true; if Ka Tanging had not been so adamant, the trial would never have been brought. I remember that when he talked about me, the prosecutor said I had "connived and abetted" the crime and was a full accomplice.

Ferdinand Marcos had joined our defense team. He was a young lawyer in his twenties, but already rather famous. He gave the opening statement in our behalf.

He argued that the defendants should not even be accused of murder, for Dr. Gabriel was a collaborator with the Japanese, a traitor who had committed the serious crime of treason. He said that Dr. Gabriel had been found guilty by the guerrilla military court, *in absentia*, during the first year of the Japanese occupation. He waxed eloquent on the theme that Dr. Gabriel, because he collaborated with the Japanese from the onset of the occupation, was responsible for the suffering and death of many people in Paranaque. Marcos claimed that Dr. Gabriel had been on the "Most Wanted List" of the guerrillas during the entire war. This was not a case of murder, he said, but simply a case of carrying out the sentence that Dr. Gabriel so well deserved.

That was the meat of what Attorney Marcos said. He spoke for about half an hour, extemporaneously, with no notes, like a veteran trial lawyer. He spoke slowly, at an even pace, with a subtle smile. His soothing baritone voice lilted easily, speaking gently as if he were explaining the obvious, stressing important points subtly but clearly. I cannot remember all he said, but I can't forget the way he sounded and looked and carried himself. He was young, extremely handsome, very slim, and appeared very tall (though he was only about five-foot seven). He wore a well-tailored, dark blue suit, white shirt, a narrow black tie, and a striking monogrammed tie clip.

Marcos always appeared well dressed, and he always spoke with authority and that subtle smile playing about his lips—as if he knew the truth and was patiently waiting for everyone else to understand.

As I said, I did not pay close attention to most of the trial. I do remember my own testimony, of course.

The prosecutor asked me, under oath, what I did upon arriving in Paranaque from Imus, on the day Dr. Gabriel was shot. I told the court all about my conversations with the mayor, including the "surgery" on my boil that allowed me to fall asleep subsequently.

He asked if I had left the car during the time we were parked in front of the guerrilla headquarters. I said, "Yes." The prosecutor then asked where I went and where the doctor was at that particular instant. I told the court that we both went to urinate. He asked if we went inside the headquarters to urinate, to which I responded, "No." The next question was where we went to urinate.

I thought this was getting silly and embarrassing, but I hesitantly answered that we went into the bushes, side by side. He then asked at what point, during the time the car was parked in front of the headquarters, did we relieve ourselves. I told the court that I could not remember exactly, but it must have been shortly after we got there.

He asked how far the headquarters was from the street, whether I had seen any persons other than the defendants, and whether there were other guerrillas guarding or watching or keeping an eye on us. I responded that no one kept an eye on us. No one even said,"Don't let him get away." He then asked why I did not drive away. He said that had I done that, I could have saved the life of the mayor.

I gave the court a long response. I started saying that neither the mayor nor I had any inkling that he would be killed. Had I known that his life was in jeopardy, there was a good possibility that I would have tried to save him. I did not know at the time that he needed saving. Killing a big man like Dr. Juan, the renowned mayor and a tower of respectability, was unthinkable for an organization like the Hunters, which had members and sympathizers from the highest classes and professions—so I really didn't think it. Yes, the thought crossed my mind, but it was too ludicrous to take seriously, so I didn't. No one had told me what we were doing with the mayor. I did not even know that he was wanted by the guerrillas.

I wound up my statement by saying that, if I had known then what I knew now, I would have let the mayor go, we would not be in the courtroom today, and the lawyers would be unemployed. The judge looked unhappy when I said that, and the room filled with laughter.

After I answered a lot more of the prosecutor's frivolous questions, I was excused and was told that I could be called later.

The trial lasted for days, but everyone knew that Dr. Juan Gabriel had been killed by the guerrillas. A single word, the foregone conclusion, could encapsulate the long, dragging trial: Guilty. The only question was which of the defendants had done what. The prosecutor, on behalf of the plaintiff, wanted to prove to the court that all seven defendants were murderers, equally responsible for the death of the mayor.

My only hope was that I had only been the driver and an unwitting guard, that I had not known what we were up to, that I had not even been a vigilant guard—I had not thought of myself as a guard at all. I could hope they would believe the truth, that I had only gone along because I knew the operation would take me near Stella's home and let me see her again.

What came out, in the course of the trial, was that when Dr. Juan had been tried *in absentia* in guerrilla court in 1944, Pareng Tangol had been given the task of carrying out the death sentence. He had not been able to do so during the Japanese occupation, and he took the liberation as an opportunity to fulfill the mission. When we arrived in Paranaque from Imus, and Dr. Juan and I were in the car outside the guerrilla headquarters, there was an argument inside about whether to carry out the sentence, now that the Japs were gone. It was not clear exactly what went on, but it seemed that only four people insisted on carrying out the penalty. Those four—Pareng Tangol, Dwight Velasco, Peping Pangat, and Caring Ison—did exactly that.

Pareng Tangol was found guilty and sentenced to life imprisonment without parole.

Dwight Velasco, Peping Pangat, and Caring Ison were found guilty of firing the shots that killed Dr. Gabriel. All four men served about seven years in prison before Jim Ferrer and others in the guerrillas were in government positions powerful enough to set them free.

The three others—Pareng Nardo, Mike Bernabe, and me—were exonerated, and the charges against the John Does were dismissed for lack of evidence.

Many years later, in about 1990, I happened to run into Dwight Velasco in Los Angeles, at a popular car repair shop, California Z, which was owned by a Filipino. He and I had lunch, and he told me that when the three trigger men were in the process of blindfolding the mayor, Dr. Juan begged and pleaded with them not to harm him. He was shaking and trembling, pleading that he would do anything they wanted, that he was a family man with a wife and two young children he loved dearly, that he had not done anything to justify what they were doing to him. When his hands were tied behind his back, and he realized he was to die, he changed his demeanor. He became dignified and quiet. He told his killers that he hoped they knew what they were doing. He offered the wish that God might bless them in spite of their misdeed. They took him to the backyard of the house, next to the toilet. He stood there very erect and brave, praying. The three gunmen stayed inside the headquarters and, through an open window, fired simultaneously, in a long volley of shots. Dwight said Dr. Juan maintained great dignity and died a quick, sudden death. When he was pronounced dead, they hurriedly buried the body right there, next to my favorite outhouse, in a shallow grave.

Dr. Juan was a brave man. I hate that I was a part of his death, unwitting though I was. I did not think then, and I do not think now, that he deserved to die.

Chapter Nine

Clinging to a Dream, Alone

After Stella's death and my trial, I could not find a place of peace. Everyone knew about my trial for the murder of Dr. Gabriel—there were rumors that I was one of the trigger men and had gotten away with it. Everyone knew about Stella. Some people were still curious about my escape from my kidnappers and the deal we had made with the culprits. Wherever I went, I was the object of curiosity, interest, pity, some suspicion, and even a measure of admiration.

I poured myself into my college studies. I was obsessed with my dream of going to America. My grades had slipped during Stella's death and my trial. Even as I tried harder to study, though, I could not tear myself away from the consolations of gambling and sports. When I was gambling or playing ball, I forgot, for awhile, my troubles. I had also started drinking, but just socially.

My favorite hangout was Maria's Refreshment Parlor in Don Galo, owned by Pilar Valentino's cousin Maria. Pilar came to the Parlor on weekends to help out. Whenever I was at Maria's Parlor, I could not help but talk and talk and talk about my kidnapping, my trial, Stella, my studies, my dream of America, over and over. I couldn't help talking—it was like a compulsion. Pilar always listened avidly.

I had not lost interest in women, but I had no room in my heart for a new love. Many, many months had passed since the violin soloist had played Stella's arrangement of Franz Schubert's *Serenade*, but the sound was still in my mind. Whenever I met an attractive woman, my mind went back to Stella and compared the two. I would lose interest in the woman and not pursue her.

Pilar caught my eye, though, as she listened so closely to all I had to say. I was not sure if she was interested in my story or just in me. I intentionally threw some flirtatious eye contacts at her, and she always responded with encouraging glances and a lovely smile. I was interested, and I talked with my friends about her. My friends kept saying that Stella was already in the other world, life must go on, Pilar could be your savior—that sort of thing. No one but me thought I should still be pining for Stella. Still, the sound of the violin playing the *Serenade* would not leave me alone.

Pilar and I were both going to school in Manila, so meeting each other was convenient. We developed a very close friendship. We enjoyed each other's company and spent many hours together. She conversed very intelligently, with clear, witty, logical opinions. She was very bright. We loved to go to the movies.

I could not settle down and give her my attention. I was gambling, smoking, and even drinking occasionally. Mahjong was very addictive. I was very good at it and would win most of the time, but then I would blow my winnings on celebrations with friends. After playing mahjong, I would go with friends to cockfights. I would not—really, could not—give Pilar my time and energy. She was very unhappy with me.

I was going through money like water. My parents gave me an allowance, and I had my winnings from gambling, but that was not enough. Since I had served the country during the war as a guerrilla, the Philippine Veterans Board was paying for my education. I did not tell my parents that—I took their money to pay for my education and spent the government money on my bad habits. This went on for about two years, until my father happened to run into Jaime Ferrer one day. Amang asked Jim why I was not getting the G.I. Bill of Rights to pay for school—you remember that Jim headed up the Philippines Veterans Board. Jim told him that, in fact, I was getting the school benefits.

My father confronted me. That was the blessing I needed. I cut back my social life, including my friendship with Pilar, drastically. I put all my energies into my studies. I also began corresponding with Ed Wadarsky, who was now a civilian in Chicago, for advice about American schools.

Pilar and I did not really break up our relationship. She was just busy pursuing her education, and I was preoccupied with my personal problems. I really liked her quite a lot, but I had no space in my heart, so we drifted apart. We saw each other from time to time, and I would wonder why I could not get over Stella. But the hard fact was, I could not. My deepest affections for women had gone with Stella when she died.

Near the end of my second year of engineering studies, I went to Kaka Mando's office in Manila, to ask for a favor. I was there to ask for (not borrow) some pocket money. I noticed a nice looking girl, in school uniform, getting into her chauffeur-driven, shiny, new Buick. I was impressed. I invited the driver to meet me for lunch, where I got him to give me information about the young woman. She was Mary de Guzman. She was twenty-one years old, attending the University of Santo Tomas Conservatory of Music, majoring in piano. Her family owned the building where my brother's business office was located. I got her school schedule and learned that her birthday was near.

I called her up one day when I knew she would be home. I introduced myself. "I know who you are," I said. I asked, "Have you seen me before?"

"No," she replied "Is there any resemblance between you and your brother?" She had met my very handsome brother.

"Oh, yes," I replied. "Our mannerisms are identical. We both talk with the Paranaque accent."

We had a nice, long conversation, and I asked her for a date. She accepted happily, and we made plans to meet in a coffee shop.

When we met, she knew right away who I was. I suspected that she was a bit disappointed, for I was not as good looking as my brother. Her first words, though, were, "You are much taller than your brother," which was a very nice thing to say.

"And much darker, too," I added, getting right to the heart of the matter. She was much lighter than I was, and skin color was always an issue in our country. The elite mostly had light complexions.

We hit it off, though, right from the start. I developed the habit of going to my brother's office almost every day. I started working for my brother to earn some pocket money, and I did all my studying there. I stopped gambling, concentrating more on my studies. From Kaka Mando's office, I could hear Mary playing the piano, which reminded me of Stella. Mary was going for a degree in music, majoring in piano, exactly as Stella had been doing.

I sent her a present, a piece of music, Richard Addinsell's *Warsaw Concerto*. I had it bound in leather, with "To Mary, from Rudy," printed in gold lettering on the cover. As soon as she received it, she began playing it on the piano.

When we went out a few days later, she surprised me by handing me a birthday card and a box of candy. I had not told her the date of my birth; she would not tell me how she found out. I figured it out, though, just a bit later—Kaka Mando threw me a surprise party, to which Mary had been invited.

For all of that, I really could not sustain enough undivided attention to get my relationship with Mary off the ground, at first. Our romantic relationship did not really get started until about a year later, near the beginning of my final year of school. Once our relationship turned romantic, though, it quickly blossomed.

By the time I finished school, the possibility of marriage was a topic of conversation, between Mary and me and within my family. My parents did not think I was ready for it, but Kaka Cely, my older sister, liked Mary immensely—she even chose Mary to be the godmother of her first daughter—and liked the idea of my marrying her. I was quite conflicted.

I liked the fact that Mary was a pianist, but hearing her ineffable music always reminded me of Stella. I could not help thinking, "Who would I choose, if Stella were alive?" I knew I would pick Stella, and I feared that would be a problem. Stella was history, and I had Mary, with all her fine qualities; but I feared that with Mary, I would always be aware that she was really my second choice. And truth to be told, I also had Pilar on my mind. I liked her very much.

I was also feeling insecure about the whole idea of marriage. Though I had finished school with honors, I had not yet taken the test for the engineering license, and I had no experience. With no license and no experience, a good job was out of the question. Also, I did not want to follow the footsteps of Kaka Mando, who had gotten married before he was really ready. Even though he was married, he continued fooling around. It was a very unhappy situation. He made his wife so miserable. They constantly fought. That was not the kind of life I would like to lead. He had married before he was ready to settle down. I did not want to make the same mistake.

The dream of going to America was still first with me, and Stella was still woven into that dream. Since I did not ardently desire to marry Mary, I decided to go to America, if at all possible. If that did not work out, marriage was "Plan B." If it came to Plan B, I would have to decide whether to marry Mary or pursue Pilar seriously.

Actually, it became even more complicated than that. My mother's dear friend, Nanang Sisay, was trying to match me with Tellie Pascual, the daughter of her first cousin, who was three years younger than I—prime marriage age, for women in the Philippines, in those days. Nanang Sisay visited my mother many times a week, and she often brought up the subject of "Rudy and Tellie." My mother would put her off, speaking of my interest in Mary and my devotion to the memory of Stella.

Every time I saw Nanang Sisay, she would say, "The mango fruit is already ripe, ready to be picked. What are you waiting for?" I would laugh and say, "Why would I want to be turned down? Besides, I have a girlfriend."

The Pascual family was the wealthiest in Paranaque and one of the wealthiest in the country. They were landed, the term used for people with vast amount of properties, owning most of Paranaque. Tellie's older brother, Dario, was a good friend of mine—he and I were together during the war. I had been to their house many times and had certainly noticed Tellie. She was sweet, soft-spoken, quite lovely, and very charming. If I had been really interested in marriage, she would have been quite a catch.

When I finished college, we had a double celebration at home, a dinner dance, for my graduation and for the christening of Kaka Cely's first daughter, Jo Ann. Mary, the baby's godmother, was exquisitely dressed and so beautiful. Tellie Pascual (and her sister) were present, to my surprise.

In the course of the evening, I danced with both Pascual sisters. To my astonishment, Tellie was quite encouraging of my affections, we might say. I was quite taken with her. As the evening progressed, I spent so much time with Tellie that Mary asked my sister, "Who is that woman who has captured Rudy's attention?" Mary was not happy.

The next few months were very confused. I kept seeing Mary, though our relationship became rather troubled, and also began seeing Tellie, though our relationship never became physical.

I could not comprehend what was going on with me. Tellie was always in my mind. I said I just wanted to be friends with her, for I did not want to get into the same situation with her that I was in with Mary. Mary and

Tellie had so many things in common. They were both very good looking and charming. They were both from very good families and very well to do. They were of the same age. And I still felt strongly about Pilar and saw her once in awhile.

If you wonder why all this was on my mind so much, I was twenty-seven, well into the age when a Filipino man was supposed to be getting married, especially one with a college degree.

All the while, I kept thinking about Stella. If only she were alive, if only, if only—I would have had no quandary at all.

I was on the phone with Tellie when my younger brother handed me a letter from the Board of Professional Engineers. I excused myself to read the letter. I screamed as soon as I read the first word—"Congratulations." When I had finished reading it, I got back to Tellie. I told her exuberantly that I had passed the examination for civil engineers. She was surprised—I had not told her, or many other people, that I had even taken the exam. She asked what was next for me. I told her that I would be looking for a job in Manila.

My parents were so happy to hear that I had passed the exam. They were so happy to have a son who was a civil engineer. I was the first one in Don Galo, maybe even in the whole town of Paranaque. That warranted a celebration.

We arranged a party, to be held at our home, of course. We invited all our friends and relatives, and almost all came. Mary and Tellie both took part. Pilar was out of town.

It was, as usual, a dinner dance. I made it a point not to drink. With Mary and Tellie both there, though, the stage was set for trouble. As you can imagine, they did not like each other. Though I honestly believe I did not pay Tellie any special attention, Mary confronted me sternly about her. I told Mary that Tellie was just a friend, which—strictly defined—was the truth. Tellie and I were not lovers, despite my feelings for her, and I had never told her how I felt.

Luckily for me, the point became moot. While the party was in progress, a cablegram from the University of California at Berkeley arrived. I was accepted! I could go to America and forget all this confusion. I was off the hook.

With this new cause for celebration, cases of San Miguel beer appeared, and they just kept coming in. My intention not to drink vanished. The ladies left shortly before midnight, but the men partied until nearly sunrise. That was the first time I was ever called an "inebriate." It would not be the last.

I had a couple or three months before heading for America, and I enjoyed them immensely. With Tellie and Mary, things rocked along as they had for some months, but I had no need to worry about settling the question. With Pilar, it became obvious that we had no romantic future—she had no interest in hanging around waiting to see if I finally got serious about her. She had her own life to live.

We planned a going away party for my adventure to Berkeley—but then came a letter that I had been accepted at Stanford, my first choice.

I decided to go to Stanford, which was much more prestigious in those days. The date for the "*La Despedida* Farewell Party" was hurriedly moved up—the school year started much earlier at Stanford than Berkeley.

The farewell party was well-attended, in spite of the short notice. All my friends were there. I had a great time, in a way, but my friends noticed that something was bothering me. They would ask, and I would just say, "Oh, no—everything is wonderful." I did not tell them, but I could not get Stella out of my mind. Our going to America for my education was the dream Stella and I had loved to talk about. This was what we had hoped for, planned, built our images of our lives around. The dream was about to materialize, but there was no Stella. All evening, I kept wishing she were alive. She could not be present, but her memory stayed with me that whole evening.

Chapter Ten

A Student in America

I was on a roll. I had finished college, and that was a big deal for me. I had passed the engineering examination, and that was also a big deal. I had been accepted at both Berkeley and Stanford, two very big deals. I had been exonerated of the murder of Dr. Juan, and I felt so good about having pardoned my kidnappers in obedience to my mother's wishes. And I was going to America.

My flight was scheduled for the day after the farewell party, so that I would not miss orientation, registration, and the first day of school. Lots of people came to the Manila International Airport to see me off. Someone handed me a copy of *The Manila Times* with my small photo and a short paragraph saying that I was bound for America to pursue graduate studies.

I had such mixed feelings. I was happy to be going to America, but sort of afraid, for I did not know a soul where I was going. I kept thinking of how I could have married Pilar or Mary or Tellie. Stella occupied my mind more than any one else. She should have been going with me.

I flew in the newest airplane that Philippine Air Lines had just acquired, a DC-10. Never before had I even seen the inside of an airplane. The flight from Manila to Guam to Honolulu to San Francisco was turbulent most of the way. I was at the back of the plane with the economy fare. Fortunately, I did not get sick like many other passengers.

We were given a fancy souvenir for crossing the International Dateline—I kept it and still have it fifty years later. For me, this flight was a big deal. That was August 29, 1951.

I was very happy getting off the airplane—America! It was almost sundown, and the air was cold—so very different from the steamy tropical heat of Manila. Inside the terminal were so many people, mostly Filipinos meeting arriving passengers. They happily hugged and kissed, talking loudly and exuberantly in Tagalog. My spirits quickly collapsed; there was nobody there to meet me. I kept looking around, searching, hoping to see someone I might know or recognize, but no such luck. I felt so sad and alone.

I scarcely knew what to do. I was so downhearted. Most of the passengers had already left the terminal, but I was almost paralyzed with sadness. Then I saw Stella—or so I thought, suffering the cruel trick your mind plays when you long for someone who is gone. I had no thought of Mary or Pilar or Tellie. Just Stella. I was so lonely, and the cold, breezy, Autumn air of San Francisco did not help.

I got stern with myself. I told myself, "I have to pull myself together. Stella would not want me ruining this chance. I've got to meet adversity head-on, with a positive attitude. This is the land of opportunity; I've got to give it a good shot."

And so I did.

I got out my instructions from the university and found the bus they told me to take to Palo Alto. During the bus ride—which took about an hour, I think—I opened a letter my father had handed to me as I boarded the airplane in Manila, with instructions to open it only when I had reached California. Such a warm, loving letter! The meat of it said, "You always have to work hard. If you fail, never give up—just keep working hard. Never divert from the Ten Commandments."

I stayed in a Palo Alto hotel for the night. The next morning, my "sponsor," a volunteer student named Claire, met me to get me settled. Her first task was to take me to my dormitory at the Stanford Village, which was about two miles from school. Then she helped me enroll and showed me around the school. What a humongous and beautiful campus! I was enchanted.

While I was paying my fees, I learned that all students were encouraged to attend all football home games, and that I was supposed to buy season tickets. I balked—I knew nothing about American football, and I was nervous about money. Claire told me to relax—the season ticket was only four dollars, for all eight games, and she would take me and explain the game. She even volunteered to pay for the tickets. Once she said all that, I bought the tickets myself. Claire turned out to be a good teacher about football—I became hooked on the game, as I remain to this day. In fact, the next year I went to the Rose Bowl in Pasadena, with four school mates, when Stanford played Michigan on New Year's Day. We drove all day from Palo Alto to Pasadena, then stayed all night along the parade route, waiting for the Rose Parade. Stanford lost, but I saw the beauty and the uniqueness of Pasadena. I fell in love with it.

Claire proved to be a Godsend—she was so kind and compassionate and helpful. Indeed, I began to believe that Someone was watching over me, a faith I had lost when Stella died. Claire and I became wonderful friends. She was so kind, and so extremely helpful, that sometimes she made me feel embarrassed. She was a very sincere, religious person, and she called me every day to see how I was doing. She did some typing for me and drove me around whenever I needed a ride, until I got my own car.

She was a senior in college, majoring in economics, about twenty or twenty-one years old when we met. I once asked her if all girls from Boston, where she had been born and raised, were like her. She said, "Yes," but I doubted her answer. She had an Irish background and talked with the Boston accent. She liked my accent and said I talked like a French person.

Claire helped me deal with my early encounters with racism. In the Philippines, I had certainly experienced Americans' patronizing attitude toward Filipinos, but I had been part of the majority, and part of one of the respected classes. In America, I began to learn what discrimination really felt like. At first, when white people acted badly toward me for no obvious reason, I would think there was some misunderstanding, and I would try to clear it up—leading to some unpleasant situations. The more I tried to "straighten things out," the more irritated and rude they would become. Claire helped me learn to recognize when racism, not misunderstanding, motivated their bad behavior. She helped me learn that trying to "clear up" anything was a waste of time and just made people mad. Since this was the 1950's, not the 1970's, we would simply remove ourselves from the situation.

I remember one time, for instance, when we went out dancing. Claire was a good dancer, and we were "cutting a rug," doing the jitterbug and swing and other very flashy steps. The manager of the night club came over and asked us to stop dancing. I asked for an explanation, and he said we were taking up too much room. I pointed out that the dance floor was not crowded, and we were not taking up any more room than anyone else. As the argument began to heat up, Claire put her hand on my arm and said, "Rudy, this man is a racist. He just doesn't want you dancing with a white girl. Let's go."

I had to learn to deal with racism—either to find a way around it or to get myself out of situations that could turn ugly. Claire helped me with that.

I don't know if I could have managed my new life at Stanford if my sponsor been a different person. Maybe I could have, but it would not have been as easy and enjoyable. Claire and I remained good friends even after she graduated.

Only a handful of Filipino students attended Stanford back then, and I became fast friends with many of them. Only one Filipino family lived in Palo Alto, the Madarangs, and they became regular hosts to our gang of friends. Paul Madarang was a chef, and his wife, Gloria, was a registered nurse. They had two young boys. We enjoyed their delicious Filipino food many Sundays. The regulars were Pat Rogers, Helen Mendoza, Felixberto Santa Maria, Johnny Dangcil, Moises Estioko, and me.

I did not really need a car, for I could always hitch a ride to and from school. Still, having one would be nice, and my love for cars had not slackened. In 1952, the later part of my freshman year, I bought a 1935 Chevrolet coupe for fifty dollars. Though it was eighteen years old and did not run, it had four new tires. Its owner, an army captain who had just earned his Ph.D. in structural engineering, had bought a new car, so when the Chevy coupe broke down the last time, he did not bother to have it fixed. Another student was supposed to buy it, but he could not make it run and changed his mind. I knew I could get it running—those old cars were very easy to tune up, if you knew what you were doing.

Our group had a lot of fun with my car, which we named "the African Queen," after the Humphrey Bogart movie we had seen and loved. Designed to seat two inside and two in the back rumble seat outside, it usually carried six or more of us. When I bought it, it looked so awful—an army brown color, with lots of faded spots. We really did not mind its appearance—we were just happy to have transportation for our outings—but we chipped in some money and bought a gallon of bright red paint, some sandpaper, and four two-inch brushes. We painted the car one Sunday in the backyard of the Madarangs. The car looked great, with plenty of Stanford Indian stickers all over.

We got in the habit of driving to Kearny Street in San Francisco to meet Filipino old-timers, who had come to America before the war. They worked mostly as drivers, servants, gardeners, or farm laborers. We enjoyed talking to them. Not least, we learned more about the extent of America's vast racism toward Filipinos. These visits were great fun, but they were also lessons in reality.

Helen Mendoza, the sister of a friend of mine from Manila, was working on her Ph.D. at Stanford. She was smart, upbeat, and fun to be around. She became my regular dance partner, but nothing romantic ever happened between us. I wasn't looking for love—I had other priorities for my time at Stanford. I went on lots of dates, as my finances allowed, but my studies came first.

In my first months at Stanford, both Mary and Tellie wrote to me regularly. I would respond, but my letters were short in comparison to theirs. I was really very busy with my books and going out on dates. Mary quickly—in the second or third month—complained about my succinct letters. I did not want to lie, so I told her I was busy with school and American girls. I told her she should go out with other men. I said that would be a good test whether we were really meant for each other. That was not my best idea—sort of like telling Mother Theresa to go out drinking and carousing. Mary was very much offended and responded with a one sentence letter: "Have fun." I did not hear from her again for quite a long time, despite my efforts to patch things up with her.

I kept writing notes and short letters to Tellie, but that came to a halt just a few months later. I sent her a gold Stanford bracelet in the Spring of 1952, and she returned it. She said that it was not right for her to accept it, since we were not engaged. By Filipino customs, she was correct. Soon thereafter, I learned that she was engaged to someone else. I should not have been surprised in the Philippines, a woman only has a certain amount of time to get married before she becomes "old goods." I had not spoken for Tellie, and someone else had. To tell the truth, that sort of broke my heart. Secretly, once Mary blew me off, I had decided that when I finished Stanford, I would go back to Manila and propose to Tellie.

If all of this romantic stuff sounds confused and doomed from the start, that's because it was. The truth is that I was not stupid, and if I had wanted, I could have conducted my romantic life in a more sensible, successful manner. The truth is that after Stella, no one else had really captured my heart. Yes, I was of an age to marry, and I thought I should. But no one had overcome the power Stella held in my memory.

I guess a troubled heart never acts in a pure, clear manner.

America was so much more expensive than the Philippines, and though my parents sent me an allowance that kept me in food and shelter, I wanted some pocket money to have a better social life. Early in 1952, I started working on weekends. I did gardening and some driving for wealthy retirees from Menlo Park and Atherton, next to Palo Alto. Those jobs, which I got through the school placement office initially, were plentiful. They paid a dollar-and-a-quarter per hour—ten dollars for an eight-hour day.

My first employer was Mrs. Banker, a huge lady. I remember that she was shocked and happy at how fast I worked. The first day, I mowed her large San Augustine lawn using her old lawn mower, then tilled a large area for a new garden, using a heavy pick. I worked so hard that I finished that work in no time. I asked, "What's next?" and she laughed. She told me to slow down, because she was running out of work. She asked me to get the water hose from the front yard. I could not loosen the hose, for both hands were blistered and bloody. I asked for a pair of pliers to loosen the hose. She looked puzzled, then just reached over and loosened the hose, easily, with her bare hands. I was embarrassed and told her I was ready to call it a day. I showed her my hands. She shrieked and asked, "Why didn't you wear gloves?" I told her I did not have any. She paid me ten dollars for about two hours work. I became the person she called whenever she needed yard work.

I also drove a couple who were in their late eighties. I was sort of a driver and nurse. I drove them to restaurants to eat. They could hardly walk, and part of my job called for helping them get in and out of the car, into the restaurant, and back into their house. That was a good job, for I could study while waiting outside the restaurant. It paid better, too.

Later on, I worked as a bus boy/dishwasher at the Yosemite National Park's Camp Curry restaurant on some weekends and holidays.

I could afford a fun social life once I started working, but after Tellie returned the bracelet, I found myself utterly discouraged about romance. I did nothing but study for the rest of the Spring term. Eventually, though, I recovered and started going out with American girls again. Sometime that summer, I found myself settling into one steady date, Jean Martin, a friend of Helen Mendoza whom I had dated a few times the previous Winter.

Jean was sweet, jovial, and vivacious. Jean and her sister, Rose, were both working on M.B.A. degrees at Stanford. The three of us were always going out in their 1951 Chevrolet Sedan, which had been shipped from their home in Atlanta to Palo Alto. They were from a very prominent family in Atlanta. I wasn't all that serious about Jean—I really wasn't thinking of marrying her—but I felt deep, tender feelings and admiration for her.

Jean's uncle—her mother's brother—was Walter White, who had served as Executive Secretary of the NAACP since 1931. Although African-American, he was fair-skinned, blond-haired, and blue-eyed. Having the ability to pass as a white man, he could travel incognito through the Deep South, though at great personal risk, to gather information on lynchings, disenfranchisement, and other types of racial discrimination. Mr. White wrote books about race in America, some of them becoming study material in public schools. Some of his books remain in print even today—for instance, *A Man Called White*, *Fire in the Flint*, and *How Far the Promised Land?*

The White family, all seven siblings and their children, had the same features as Mr. White, and yet they all had chosen to live as blacks. They could have crossed over from black to white, just like thousands of Americans did every year. Many black southerners who had "crossed over" were even worse than the southern whites in their hatred of blacks. The White family wanted no part of that charade. Jean's father was the C.E.O. of one of the largest black businesses in America, the Atlanta Life Insurance Company.

When I first met Jean, it did not dawn on me that she was black, for she had features of a white person. When she told me of her racial background and the story of her family, my love for her bloomed fully. Still, I had no plans for marriage.

I must not fail to tell you of Mr. and Mrs. Frank Caso, who became in essence my adoptive parents in America. The Caso family lived in Santa Cruz, an hour and a half drive from Palo Alto. I had met them when they hosted a dinner party for foreign students—something that wealthy families in the area often did. I had been to many of these meet-the-foreign-student dinners, but with the Casos, something special "clicked." They took a special liking to me, and I to them. They were so kind and helpful. I spent countless holidays and family celebrations with them. They called me their "foster son."

When I met them in 1952, they owned an Italian Restaurant in downtown Santa Cruz. Mr. Caso had won many awards for his cheesemaking and made a good bit of money from it—he was "a big cheese in cheese." He was tall and slender, with a full head of graying hair and a mustache. His wife was short and quite heavy. They were like Jack Spratt and his wife. They lived in a rambling five-bedroom, one-story house, with a basement full of aging cheese and a big yard filled with huge trees.

They had two girls and two boys. Except for the youngest boy, Frank, Jr., the children were all married and out of the house. Frank, Jr., was over twenty-one and lived with his girlfriend. The Caso children all lived around Santa Cruz, and the girls helped run the restaurant. Mrs. Caso made a point of having all her children present whenever I was invited to Santa Cruz, if at all possible, so I got to know the whole family very well.

The Casos kept me going whenever I got discouraged. I had no problems passing school tests and examinations, but I had terrible problems with writing term papers and reports. I did not have a typewriter, nor did I know how to type, and my command of the English language was far from perfect. Those reports took so much of my time that I had trouble studying for final exams. In my last quarter, I was so overworked that I considered dropping two subjects and extending my education for another term. I wasn't sure that even that would be enough. I confided to the Casos my doubts about being able to graduate. I just didn't think I would be able to submit all the term papers and pass all the finals. They augmented my father's admonition to work very hard, and they urged not to give up on even one subject. They said they would pray for me—they were very devout. I followed their advice, and with their moral support and encouragement, I passed all my courses.

When my school adviser told me that my application to graduate had been approved, I immediately called my parents in Manila, my foster parents in Santa Cruz, Claire (she had graduated taken a job in San Francisco), and my girlfriend, Jean. I sat down and wrote a letter of thanks to Ed Wadarsky, who had set me on the path to this great accomplishment.

In June, 1953, at Stanford's football stadium, Mr. and Mrs. Caso stood in for my parents at graduation. (Amang and Inang had not been able to work out the logistics to come on short notice—I had been so afraid I would not graduate that I had not told them to get ready. When I got word that I would really graduate, it was too late.) Claire came up for the occasion, and of course, Jean was there. I was so happy. The Casos took us out to dinner, then I went with them to Santa Cruz, where I slept for two days straight. I remained close to Mr. and Mrs. Caso for the rest of their lives.

Shortly thereafter, I accepted a job in San Francisco with Bechtel Corporation, while Jean and Rose took jobs in New York. That was fine with me. I was ready to start my life in America, on my own, free to find my personal path.

Chapter Eleven

Married, then Not

Now, in the summer of 1953, I had nothing major troubling me for the first time since Japan invaded the Philippines. I was a graduate of Stanford, an engineer with a new job at Bechtel, living in San Francisco. I had a brand-new car, an income, and a new life. Stella entered my mind less often, and she never stayed for long. I was enjoying the bachelor life. Bechtel occasionally sent me to their New York branch for short assignments, which allowed me to see Jean. I always looked forward to that. Rose, Jean's sister, joined us whenever she was free. I was on an expense account when working in New York, and I "lived it up" first class—and big time. I loved to dance, and so did Jean and Rose. We danced jitterbug and *cha cha*. The three of us "painted the town red," as the saying goes. Cheap nights of hot dogs, hamburgers, pizza, or spaghetti were things of the past.

The fly in the ointment was racism. Even in New York City, racism was rampant in the 1950s. In late 1953 in New York, I was staying at Grand Hotel, not far from Grand Central, on 42nd street. Jean and Rose lived in the Village around 14th and Broadway. I tried to rent a room from a very nice residence place near them, but the manager told me there were no rooms available—he said the "Vacancy" sign was a mistake and would be removed soon. When I told Jean and Rose about it, Rose went into a slow burn. She went to the residence inn and asked for a room. (Remember, Rose and Jean looked white.) They showed her a room; she then asked if she had anything nicer. They showed her three other rooms. Then she dropped the subterfuge and gave them a piece of her mind. The manager apologized and had agreed to take me, but I refused to stay there anyway. I did not want to be in a place I knew was racist.

Once I had adjusted to my new city and new job, I took an apartment of my own—when I had first come to San Francisco, I had taken a room in a boarding house. In that Fall of 1953, I got word from Mary de Guzman that she was coming to San Francisco with a symphony orchestra, and she wanted to see me. I was very happy to hear from her, and I told her to stay with me while she was in town. She did, bringing one of her friends along.

Mary still wanted to marry me. Quite frankly, if I had been at all interested in marriage, I would have welcomed that. Even at this point, Mary was my first choice as a marriage partner, since Stella was dead. I told her, though, that I did not want to be married and that I had a girlfriend in New York. I remember that she cried.

In the midst of that, I received a call from Bechtel's project manager in New York. He wanted me in New York as soon as possible, for a rush job. I called Jean to tell her I was coming. I left Mary and her friend in my apartment and headed out.

Jean and Rose met me at Laguardia Airport in New York. We were all very happy, but I could sense that there was something bothering Jean. We went out to dinner, where Jean was unusually quiet. Even in her silence, she seemed perturbed.

Later that evening, Jean told me that she had gone to the doctor the day before and found out she was pregnant.

I suggested another test from a different doctor. Jean took my advice, but the results were the same. I told Jean that I wanted the pregnancy aborted. She was afraid of abortion and ruled that out altogether. We spent many weeks looking into our options. Jean wanted to get married, move to San Francisco, and raise the baby there.

I did not like that idea. I was not ready, mentally or financially, to settle down. I was only beginning to feel free of the war, its aftermath, and the loss of Stella. My salary was not very much, but it was enough to live comfortably as a bachelor. I was having fun and did not want to be tied down.

I tried, with all my powers of persuasion, to convince Jean to go for an abortion and let us enjoy life for a while longer—all to no avail. She was unfazed and resolute. She wanted the baby, whether married or not married, with or without me.

That really did not leave me any choice. My only other alternative was to walk out of her life. Suddenly, Stella was back on my mind, and I was tormented with having lost her. Just as I had done with Mary and Pilar and Tellie, I found myself comparing Jean to Stella. And I found myself thinking of Mary, knowing that if I had been planning to marry anyone right then, she would have been the one.

"Stop it," I told myself. "I cannot cop out on Jean. I love Jean, and I love her even more because I am a minority, just like her. What else do I want in a wife than what Jean offers?"

I could not bear the thought of another loss, to compound the loss of Stella. I had to go along with whatever Jean wanted. We were both suffering, and I felt so sorry for her and so guilty.

Jean and I asked Rose for help. We wanted to get married without telling their family about the pregnancy. They called their parents in Atlanta. They told them that I was a school mate at Stanford and that I was a Filipino. The family was outraged. They did not want their daughter marrying a Filipino. They would not give their permission for the marriage.

That shocked me, but it offered me hope. Since her parents would not approve of our marriage, I thought Jean might change her mind. I tried to convince her that marrying against her family's wishes was a bad idea and that having the baby out of wedlock was at least as bad. She stubbornly reiterated that she would not terminate the pregnancy, that she would keep the baby whether I liked it or not.

I seriously considered just walking out of her life. I would think of Stella and compare Jean to her. But that was wrong; I would not let myself think that way. I got very stern with myself.

Since her parents would not approve of our marriage, Jean wanted to get married secretly. We went to New York City Hall for a marriage license, and we were married by a judge in Yonkers. We headed for Atlantic City to "celebrate." It was not a happy celebration. Though we were man and wife, our problems were far from over.

Jean went to see her parents In Atlanta. She did not tell them we were already married; she went to convince them to allow us to be married, in a proper wedding, with guests and a minister.

In their first discussions, her parents tried very hard to persuade her not to marry me. They said that if the reason was pregnancy, they would help her with an abortion. Jean denied being pregnant, insisting she was in love with me and wanted me for her husband. She reminded them that she was over twenty-one and free to make her own choice. She was fully aware of all the things they had done for her, she said, but her mind was made up. Her mother stayed angry and cried often, while her father stayed cool and aloof. At one point, Jean almost gave in and went for the abortion, but ultimately she held her resolve. She wanted the baby.

Jean kept me informed by phone. I was knocking my brains out worrying what to do. We were married, but the thought of being tied down still bugged me. I loved Jean, and I had convinced myself that being married to her was fine. I thought that if she would only go for an abortion, the big problem would disappear. We liked and loved each other, and we could have a lot of fun without the responsibility of a child.

Late in the second day of her visit with her parents, Jean called me up to tell me, happily, that her parents had changed their minds. They would give her the wedding she wanted. She told me to make flight plans to Atlanta. Rose was summoned to come home to prepare for the wedding. Meanwhile, Jean went to New York to quit her job.

I flew to Atlanta and checked into a hotel. Rose met me and introduced to me to their parents for the first time. Mrs. Martin was not only very nice and pleasant but also very charming. Jean's father, Eugene Martin, was a happy and inquisitive person. Jean's aunt, Madeline White, had a stunning beauty and looked very Swedish, with very light blue eyes. She was the youngest of the White family.

They all seemed to like me once they met me. I was not a talker, more of a listener. I would respond to their questions and add some little jokes. I thought they liked that. I told them everything about my family in the Philippines when they asked.

Then they asked me to play some music on their grand piano. I had quit playing the piano when Stella died, so I told them that I was never a good player and had not played for many years. They insisted, saying not to worry if I make any mistakes. I suppose it says a lot that, in the home of my new parents-in-law, I sat down at the piano for the first time since Stella died and played Franz Schubert's *Serenade*.

Jean and I were married in their house in Atlanta, the way Jean had wanted. A small wedding, though larger than Jean would have preferred—they had so many friends and relatives, and even though they hurt some people's feelings by not inviting them, the place was packed. None of my family could make it, on such short notice. Jean looked so beautiful in her white dress. Rose, dressed in red, was just as beautiful. The minister of their family church officiated. The event was a great success.

I had sold my new car, since I knew we needed money to start our married life. The family gave us the '51 Chevy that Jean and Rose had driven while at Stanford. Jean and I packed the Chevy with all the wedding presents it would hold (the rest were sent by mail) and headed out on our honeymoon. We had planned three weeks on the road from Atlanta to San Francisco.

Along the way we stopped at beaches, zoos, parks, and lakes. We went to night spots along the way, wining and dining and dancing. Oddly enough, given my anxieties before the wedding, we felt so free. This marriage thing was not so bad. We were enjoying the trip so much that I called my office and got a two week extension to my honeymoon. Jean called her parents almost every day during the trip—a sign of things to come, though I did not realize it then.

After a six-week leave, I went back to work. Jean loved my apartment in San Francisco, especially after she had rearranged the furniture to her taste. We unpacked the wedding gifts and Jean sorted the presents. We had duplicates and even triplicates of ordinary items, like alarm clocks, mixers, pressure cookers, dishes, and pots and pans. We also had received an enormous amount of cash.

Jean started working for Union Oil Company shortly after we arrived. With both of us working, we were making enough money to enjoy married life. We were going out weekends and taking short trips around San Francisco.

After a few months, though, eight months into her pregnancy, she felt terrible at work one day and had to go home. She stayed home the next day, and early in the afternoon she called me to come home right away. I did, and I took her to the hospital. Our child was born prematurely and lived just one day. We named the boy Rudy Hernandez de Lara.

We were both broken-hearted, especially Jean. To be honest, I felt some relief; but by this time, I had begun envisioning having a child, and I was very sad when Rudy died. Jean's great pain really tore me up. For both of us, though, the child's demise solved one problem: We had never admitted to Jean's parents that she had lied to them, that in fact we had gotten married because she was pregnant. Now we did not have to let them know about that at all. They never knew about the birth and death of their first grandchild.

We had a couple of very good years. With both of us working, we were making plenty of money. We were living it up and still saving. We both had plenty of friends, and we went to a lot of parties. We rode to work together every day—our offices were only a few blocks apart—and often met at lunch to "brown bag it" together in the car. Jean was a great cook, a skill she had learned from her mother, and a wonderful homemaker. I had become an American citizen, something that made me proud. Life could not have been any happier.

Jean's work had little to do with her real talents and knowledge—it was basic-level bookkeeping, far beneath her. We had money in the bank. We decided she should stop work and have another baby. In late 1957, Rudy Martin de Lara, whom we call Marty, was born. He was a nice looking boy, and we were crazy about him. Our little family had a wonderful time together.

Our living standard did not decline, though Jean was not working and we had a son. I didn't think much about it at first, but when I became puzzled and commented on it, Jean told me the truth. Without my knowledge, she was getting money from her parents—more money, in fact, than she had made working.

Over time, I grew tired of dealing with racism. Ironically, in my marriage to Jean, people usually assumed she was white and I wasn't. We learned quickly that she could do things I couldn't. For instance, shortly after Marty was born, we decided on the spur of the moment to drive from San Francisco to Atlanta, to show Marty to his grandparents. We also had just bought a new Pontiac Starchief—the big, expensive one—and the idea of a road trip seemed like a great adventure. We left San Francisco one Friday after work and stayed in Las Vegas for the evening. The next day, we drove to Dallas—where three nice hotels turned me down, saying that they were full, in spite of their "Vacancy" signs. At the third one, I asked Jean to go back in and ask for a room. She got one, and I joined her and Marty. The same thing happened around Jackson, Mississippi, and in Birmingham, Alabama. In Atlanta, her family put our fancy Pontiac in the garage and told us to drive their ten-year-old Oldsmobile. They said it would not be safe for a dark-skinned man to be seen around Atlanta in our expensive new car, especially with a woman who looked white. Remember, this was the 1950's.

Though I liked what I was doing at Bechtel, it had become clear that a Filipino faced serious impediments to advancement there. Even after I had passed my California professional engineering exam, I was working under white boys who had no professional credentials, four or five years after I had started with the company. My salary lagged way behind even those white people doing exactly the same job, and I saw white men with less experience than me promoted ahead of me. Sometimes, the situation was just a joke—I would really be running the job, for all practical purposes, while answering to some white guy who was nominally my boss but did not really know what he was doing, while I was solving problems for white engineers who made more money but could not do without my expertise.

Another Filipino engineer, a friend of mine, suggested we go back to the Philippines and go into partnership. Though I loved America, I really believed I was at a dead end, so I accepted his proposal. Jean, who certainly knew racism well, agreed; we decided to try to make a life in the Philippines.

In the Spring of 1959, I went ahead of Jean and Marty to arrange the house we would call "home" in Don Galo—a three bedroom house, facing the beach of the Manila Bay, the beach where I had spent so much of my youth. My old friends and family began throwing "welcome back" parties. These went on for more than three months, even after Jean and Marty had arrived.

One thing I had not counted on in returning to Don Galo: the place was soaked with memories of Stella. Looking back, I suppose an astute observer would have known I had never come to terms with her death. Maybe what I called, "*Bahala na*," really was denial. I was stunned to find myself in anguish over her. I cannot emphasize strongly enough that I was totally, totally surprised to find myself consumed with memories and pain.

I could not get her out of my mind. I started partying, drinking, and gambling from the day I arrived, trying to stop the torment. "That is all past," I told myself. "Look how much fun I am having now!" I guess I knew I was kidding myself, but I just kept drinking and gambling and partying, pretending it was fun, even after my family had arrived. I could not stop.

Going out nightly, I had problems getting up in the mornings to go to work. I spent some time with my family and took some trips, but the excitement of gambling and cockfighting did more to get Stella off my mind. Jean knew the problem, but she was miserable.

I loved Jean and Marty, and at first, with great efforts, I would stop my carousing for a few days at a time. After awhile, though, I gave up trying. I hardly took my family around. I did more gambling and drinking. There were no other women involved—just the thought of Stella. I even refused to see Mary de Guzman the whole time I was there—Mary had stayed close to Kaka Cely and tried to get Cely to arrange a get-together with me, but I did not want to make my life even worse by risking involvement with another woman.

We had plenty of money saved. My mother had loaned us one of her well-trained house maids, who did the food shopping, cooking, housework, and baby sitting. We had a lovely house. My family loved Jean. But I just was not there. I put Jean through Hell.

Our engineering firm received a fairly good-sized job, but I could not make it to work earlier than 10 or 11 o'clock. That was not fair to my partner, so I quit. At my younger brother Tommy's suggestion, I went into the business of importing chickens from Mindanao, a southern island of the Philippines, to Manila. That fit my terrible new lifestyle all too well. I could attend to my chicken business for a couple of hours each morning, then after lunch head to the *sabongan* for the cockfights. I could go out of town on gambling trips, plausibly telling Jean I was on business.

I was making more money than I had done as an engineer in America and the Philippines combined, and I had no boss to report to, so I could conduct my life as I pleased. But I was losing my wife.

I saw a psychiatrist, a psychologist, and a therapist from the University of the Philippines, but I could not get free. Mr. and Mrs. Caso came from

Santa Cruz for a visit, and I poured out my heart, asking for their help. They tried, but their efforts were unavailing. My gambling sickness was like walking on quick sand. The more I wanted to get out, the deeper I sank.

The only advice that seemed promising was to leave the Philippines, and I did not want to do that. I have heard that some famous writer said, "Between grief and nothing, I'll take grief." That was sort of how I felt. As painful as my memories were, I did not want to give them up. I certainly wanted to stop acting destructively, but I did not want to give up the memories that provoked my sickness.

Finally, Jean gave up. In the early Spring of 1960, she asked her mother to come to Manila to take her and Marty home to Atlanta.

Jean's mother came and stayed with us for three weeks. My mother-in-law fell in love with my parents, my family, the country, and the people. She claimed that it was the most enjoyable vacation she ever had. She could not understand why I could not settle down and make Jean happy, so we could enjoy life in the Philippines. Jean knew why. She knew the whole story.

After the three-week visit, I sadly took Marty, Jean, and her mother to the airport. Jean told me that she had done everything she knew to help, and she was very sorry to leave me. They were going to stay with her parents in Atlanta. If I decided to go back to San Francisco, all I had to do was call her and we would try to make our marriage work. She would join me and live anywhere I wanted—except the Philippines.

I stayed in Don Galo, gambling and drinking, for another two or three months. But going home intoxicated, to an empty house, was not the life I wanted. I called Jean in Atlanta and asked her to meet me in San Francisco. She agreed.

I went back to work for Bechtel. (Shortly thereafter, I transferred to their former partner, The Ralph M. Parsons Company, in Los Angeles.) My gambling and drinking sicknesses went away, once I left the Philippines. In one sense, the cure was easy; I had no trouble stopping, once I was back in

America. In another sense, the cure was terrible. I could never again stay for long in the country of my birth, without falling back into my problems.

Two years later our second son, Eugene Melchor de Lara, was born. But our happiness with Marty and Mel was short lived. I think Jean had never fully transferred her loyalty to me, and our separation had made her more reliant on her family in Atlanta. If there had ever been any hope that her first allegiance would be to me, our time in the Philippines probably killed it.

Jean wanted a nicer house than I could provide. Her parents offered to help us with the down payment and the monthly mortgage. I would not hear of it. I insisted that we buy a "fixer upper" that we could afford, and so we did. To save money, I did most of the work. New bathroom, new kitchen, new paint job, and so forth. Jean and I argued all the time. She was not working and could not stand living in the mess of a construction site. She was very angry that my refusal to take money from her parents was the only reason she did not have the house she wanted. In the midst of all that, she wanted a new car, which I could not afford, so she took money from her parents for it, in defiance of my expressed wishes.

With my income, we could live modestly but not luxuriously. When Jean wanted things, though, all she had to do was call her parents. I took that as an insult. She was my wife now, not their child. We were miserable together. In 1963, when Marty was six and Mel was two, we agreed to divorce. I realized later that it was mostly my fault. I had given her plenty of reasons to be unhappy with me. Jean took the boys and went back to her family in Atlanta.

My company offered me a chance to work in Germany and I took it, even before our divorce was final.

Chapter Twelve

Finding Myself

I suppose that the end of every failed marriage brings sadness and regret, especially when children are involved; but in reality, it mostly brings relief. Getting out of constant hostility and conflict takes away such a burden. Living like that is just bad. Worse, it kills off your hope for the future. As long as you stay in that kind of marriage, the future just looks like more of the same. Getting out of such misery, no matter who mainly caused the misery, gives you the chance to think about a happy life again. I'm not going to deny that I had a lot of pain over the end of my marriage, but I'm not going to pretend that it was not, overall, a big improvement. Why else end a marriage?

For me, the end of my marriage, whatever pain it involved, was basically a great opportunity. This is strange to think about, but I believe it is true:

In my teenage years, I had the pains of war, followed by my kidnapping, Stella's death, and my murder trial. No sooner had I gotten on my feet from all that than I found myself marrying against my true wishes. Now I had a chance to make a life of my choosing. That was a very big deal.

The chance to work in Germany was a Godsend. In Germany, I had freedom and opportunities I had never had before. In Germany, there were, for me, no ghosts. I had no obligations except those I chose willingly. In Germany, I think I came into my own for the first time since Stella's death.

After my failed marriage, I intended to enjoy life, but within my means. I had no intention of marrying again—"Been there, done that." My initial assignment to Europe was short-term, so I resolved to see as much as possible, as quickly as possible. Happily enough, with what I was earning, I could see quite a lot in quite a fine style. By now, I was a senior engineer with a good salary, and the exchange rate was four Deutschmarks for every dollar. I had a fifteen percent salary bonus and an overseas-living allowance of five hundred dollars a month. Whenever I went on an assignment outside the office in Frankfurt, the company picked up all my expenses. I was putting my normal paycheck in my savings account back in America and living on my allowances—but I could not even spend all of that!

I had taken a bit of German in college, and once I arrived in Germany I worked hard to learn the language. Within six months, I could carry on simple conversations. I found German easy to learn but hard to master. I did well enough to get around without difficulty and have relationships with Germans who spoke no English.

My life-long love of cars and my new income led me to buy a Porsche 911S Targa, which I loved driving at top speeds along the autobahn. The tailor on the ground floor of my apartment building loved me, for I had him make me beautiful three-piece suits of the finest wool whenever he had new fabrics. I took my friends for fine dinners, and I traveled all over Europe with many beautiful women. Happily, even as I lived this high life, I never went back to my drunken, dissolute ways.

The company of women came easily. I was exotic, of course, a dark Filipino. I was not bad looking, not too short, always dressed in dapper three-piece suits, an American citizen, driving an expensive German automobile. Girls loved to go out with me in my Targa. Being an engineer I had prestige, and being a spendthrift with a great income, I offered women a chance to share in my lavish life. Of course, I was a "sure ticket" to America, and I watched out to be sure women were not looking to ride on that ticket. If a girl started hinting at marriage, I hastily made my exit.

I also enjoyed my co-workers in a wonderful way. The Germans have a tradition that employees should give what they called an "*einstand* party" to celebrate special occasions—for instance, new employees gave them to celebrate being hired, and regular employees gave them if they had a birthday, bought a new car, moved to a new apartment, got engaged—whatever. As you can imagine, for a Filipino, such celebrations were second nature. The head of the office, Bill Van Ness, eventually put me in charge of all *einstand* parties. Under my watch, we had them almost every evening.

My engineering work—mostly designing and building petrochemical facilities-was very taxing mentally, and doing a good job required that I get plenty of rest. I worked very hard from eight o'clock in the morning until five in the afternoon every day, and quite often I had to take some work home after *einstand* parties during the week. Even when I went out during the week, I made it a point to get at least six hours of sleep, usually eight.

My apartment in Frankfurt and the Parsons offices were in the same building, which helped with taking good care of myself. My bedroom was actually next to my office, though they were separated by a solid wall. (I had to take an elevator from the fourth floor to the first, then another from the first to the fourth, to get back and forth between home and office.) I could go to bed at one o'clock in the morning and still be at work by eight, while getting my six hours sleep. On one occasion, I overslept—and my office mates just pounded on the wall to wake me up.

Weekends, though, from Friday night until Sunday night, were devoted to fun. My temporary assignment was extended to one year, then extended by another, and another, and another, and another—but every year I thought was my last. My intention to take in all of Europe that I possibly could never faltered. I took many trips—to Paris, Amsterdam, London, Venice, Luxembourg, all the cities of Germany, Switzerland, Italy, Spain, you name it. This was a wonderful life, a far cry from hiding in the fields with my guerilla *compadres*, fearing the *zona*.

My abilities at my job grew, and I became one of the Principal Structural Engineers for my company all over Europe. I worked in Paris, London, and other places. More than once, I saved projects that the clients were threatening to pull. As if I did not already have more money than I could spend, my good work kept getting me raises.

The quality of my work, and the crucial role I played in Parsons' projects throughout Europe, saved my skin in company politics, both from racists and from people who resented my lifestyle. There were certainly people who resented a dark-skinned engineer, and others who resented my "womanizing" and partying.

For instance, in about 1966, I got a message to come to the office of Bill Van Ness, the head of Parson's Frankfurt office. When I entered, to my surprise I found Joe Ozga and Fred Bruner waiting there. This was not good: Mr. Bruner, our chief engineer, had always been unfriendly to me. (Joe had told me once that Bruner really did not like me, to which I responded, "Joe, I would have to be stupid not to know something so obvious.") Joe Ozga had been my friend in Los Angeles, and the company had brought him to Europe on my recommendation; but he had become Mr. Bruner's ally. Bruner had made him chief structural engineer, passing me over in spite of my clear superiority in education, credentials, and experience—Joe was not even a professional, licensed engineer. Bruner, a very pious, austere man who generally seemed opposed to fun, had also put a stop to *einstand* parties within the company. He certainly liked the blue-eyed employees best, and he never revealed any interest in anything like a glamorous lifestyle.

After the usual morning salutations, I asked Bill what was going on. He asked if the stories of my womanizing and partying were true, and if my women "friends" included women from the office. This was hardly a secret, and I certainly had no shame about it, so I said, "Of course." I saw Joe and Bruner exchange knowing smiles, like "We've got him now."

However, Bill turned and asked Joe Ozga, "Isn't Rudy doing first-rate work?" Joe responded affirmatively—he could hardly have done otherwise, since all of my performance evaluations, including one less than a month prior, were excellent. Then Bill asked Joe about my work attendance and timeliness. Joe said they were fine—as, again, he could not have denied, since these were matters of record. Joe and Bruner began to get uneasy—this was obviously not the meeting they thought they had engineered!

Van Ness then pointed his index finger at Joe and Mr. Bruner, shook it in their faces, and said, "I don't want to hear any more complaints about Rudy. You know perfectly well that you cannot impugn his work. Whatever is bugging you, it has nothing to do with that. Now, what he does after work is his business, and frankly, I wish I had the social life Rudy has. Get out of my office. Goodbye." He stared them down, then turned away.

As Joe and Bruner made their awkward retreat from his office, they looked like a couple of wet hens. I strutted out like the king rooster of the barnyard.

I was lucky to have Bill Van Ness running the show during my time in Europe. He was a real go-getter, whose first priority was expanding Parsons' operations and getting the work done. He treated me well from the start. Van Ness knew how to take care of his people. For instance, at one point a major American oil company threatened to pull a job Parsons' London office was doing for them, so Van Ness told me to go quickly to London to save the job. Parsons' employees normally traveled in economy class, but since this trip came on short notice, I was booked into the executive section. I was sitting there after boarding, and I saw Van Ness coming aboard—heading for economy class. I was shocked and embarrassed—I went back to economy and insisted that he and I exchange seats. He adamantly refused. During the flight, he came up to see me, and he gave me a big wink and a smile when he saw me seated between two German ladies, exerting all my charms. After we returned to Frankfurt, when I had saved the contract in London, he sent me a thank-you note for the good job I had done in London and gave me very nice little raise.

It didn't hurt anything that Bill and his wife, June, both liked me as a person. June loved to dance, and I sometimes went to parties at their house—mostly, I think, because June loved to dance with me. With Van Ness's sophistication, eye for quality work, and personal liking of me, no one—not even Bruner, who was second in power only to Van Ness—had a chance to undermine my standing.

Though I had vowed not to marry again, I found that resolve wavering. In 1966, Ute Hamann, an engineer, joined our company, working for me. She was certainly beautiful, but more important, she was smart, witty, and sarcastic. She had no apparent interest in moving to America, so I didn't keep my guard up, as I had been careful to do with other women I'd been attracted to. I found myself developing a serious interest in Ute. I found myself thinking, "Well, if I were to marry again, Ute would be a good wife." Then, "Maybe I would like to marry Ute." I was not comparing Ute to Stella; though I had certainly not forgotten Stella, I was no longer haunted.

Jean and I had never finalized our divorce, and I had stayed in fairly close contact with her and our sons, including going to Atlanta to see the boys regularly. As I found the idea of marrying Ute coming into my mind, I began to realize that if I married her, I could lose my sons. I still loved my sons very much, and I still harbored some hope of being with them again. I was thinking, "I would marry Ute if not for my sons," but that was a big "if." I really did not like the idea of losing my sons.

During the Christmas holidays of 1966, I went to America and took Jean and the boys to Miami for a week. Jean's mother argued fiercely with Jean not to go, but as usual, Jean did just what she wanted. I had a good time with Marty and Mel, but between Jean and me nothing romantic occurred. She was there just to share the fun with the boys—nothing more.

I tried to talk Jean into giving our family another chance, but after several days of unfruitful pleading, I gave up. She was unfazed by my arguments, insisting that since our divorce, she had devoted her life to the boys and had no wish to change their life. She had no interest in marrying anyone. She had the life she wanted. She certainly intended to let the boys continue to see their father—that was good for them.

Now I knew that vexing myself over my old family was pointless. I could not have them back—but I was not going to lose contact with my boys. At the airport in Miami, I sent a telegram to Ute, asking her to marry me. When I got back to Germany, she accepted.

Arranging to marry Ute took some time. The divorce from Jean had to be finalized, and I had to get all sorts of papers in Germany to marry a German citizen, since I was American. Getting the German papers was complicated by the fact that I had been born in the Philippines, and there were discrepancies between my Filipino birth certificate and my U.S. passport. The bureaucratic process took about six months.

During that time, I was sent to Paris to be in charge of the structural work there. That was a plum assignment, one that every engineer wanted. I went to Paris by myself while Ute continued working in our Frankfurt office, but we saw each other nearly every weekend and all holidays.

We were married on June 27, 1967, in Frankfurt, and Ute officially changed her residence to Paris. On our way to Paris after the marriage, I was in such high spirits. A police car, exactly the same model Porsche that I was driving, pulled ahead of us. I wanted to have some fun, so I pulled even with him and started racing with him. I had just had my car tuned up, and it was running like a dream. The cop tried to outrun me, but I just kept increasing my speed, staying one or two car lengths ahead of him. His Porsche was not as well tuned as mine, and he could not get above about 200 kilometers per hour (125 mph)—I could easily go 230 kph (over 140mph). When it was obvious he couldn't outrun me, he waved me over to the side of the road. He walked around my car looking for some sort of violation—he even measured the height of my license plate, which was fine. My car was pristine, so he found nothing. He then told me that he was giving me a ticket for not moving to the slower lane after passing him.

I asked, "How was I supposed to do that, when you were staying right on my tail?" I started to argue, but Ute gently told me to be quiet. The cop assessed a fine of five Deutschmarks—that amounted to $1.25, U.S. I did not want to pay it, and once again I started to argue. Ute was the voice of reason—she said not to get into an ego contest with the guy. It wasn't worth the hassle. So I paid him, and we headed home to Paris.

In Paris, we stayed in an apartment on Avenue de la Opera , between the opera house and the Louvre. Within a few months, Ute got pregnant—which made both of us so very happy.

Shortly thereafter, I was asked to go to Italy to take over a big project there. Frankly, I did not really want to do it. I wanted to go back to L.A., an idea Ute approved of, to start my new family in the States. The company promised to send me back to America if I would just go to Padua to salvage a project there.

We shipped all our furniture and belongings from Paris to Los Angeles. We drove from Paris to Padua, spending a day in Monaco and some time in Milan, Florence, Venice, and a number of other cities along the way. We then spent about four months working in Padua, where Ute was already preparing, like a good mother, for the birth of our first child. She knitted sweaters and booties, and she studied books about raising and educating children. We spent a great deal of time in Venice, the most exquisite city in the world.

When I was done with my assignment in Italy, we made a trip to Egypt to see the pyramids, then we headed for the Philippines so I could introduce my new wife to my parents and family. This was my first trip back since I had wrecked my first marriage, and I was quite nervous about it. I asked my brothers and sisters to plan a full, entertaining schedule to help me stay out of trouble. They did exactly that—they planned so many parties and celebrations that I gained about thirty pounds, give or take a few!

Don Galo had changed so much, and I now had a whole set of bad memories of my bad behavior there, so that the memory of Stella did not totally consume me. There were fewer reminders of her—the beach on which we had spent so many hours was now covered with the shanties of squatters, for instance. I certainly thought of her a great deal. I made it a point, though, never to leave Ute's sight.

We stayed in the Philippines about six weeks. By the time we were ready to head for L.A., Ute was so far along in her pregnancy that Philippine Airlines refused to let her fly—it was their policy, for the safety of mother and baby, not to let women in advanced pregnancy aboard their airplanes.

I would not stand for that. To be president of the United States, a person has to be born in America, and I wanted my child to have that option! It was time to pull some strings. Since my little brother, Tommy, was a senior pilot with PAL, and my big sister, Kaka Cely, was a doctor who would vouch for my wife's safety, we were able to depart for Los Angeles in mid-July, 1968.

Epilogue

My Life

The baby, Sue Kay De Lara, came on schedule, on August 21, 1968, in the Queen of Angels hospital in Los Angeles. Sixteen months later, on December 21, 1969, came Dee Jay De Lara, in the same Hospital. With my two boys and two girls, that was just perfect for me. But then, on March 27, 1971, came Kim Marikit De Lara, our unplanned but very welcomed addition, a lovely surprise, our third daughter.

Shortly after Kim was born, I planned a big trip to Manila with Ute and our girls. Rumor had it that President Marcos intended to declare martial law, but you cannot live your life by rumors. I booked our flight with Philippine Air Lines for September 27, 1972. When Marcos declared martial law a week before we were to go, my brother Tom—the pilot with

PAL—helped us cancel our plans. I refused to bring my family to the Philippines under martial law. My friends and I had not fought for a free Philippines, only to have Marcos and his "charming" wife become the conjugal dictators. They stole billions of dollars from the country, treating the whole populace as their personal-enrichment brigade.

I had left the Philippines before Marcos became king—I mean, president—and I really did not know who he was, so far as politics went. I only knew that he had been a very brilliant young lawyer, that I admired and adored him during my murder trial, and that I felt gratitude for his help in exonerating me. Much to my regret, I supported his political campaigns from afar while I was in Europe. Knowing what I do now, I am very angry and ashamed ever to have done that.

After Cory Aquino became president, God bless her, I finally took my girls to the Philippines. They loved it so much and gave me a hard time for never taking them there before. After all, they proudly claim the fact that they are half Filipina.

For over thirty years, Ute and I have been happy. We have traveled the whole world, and we have raised a wonderful family. Shortly after Sue was born, Ute started a Montessori school of her own, which has prospered under her extraordinary management. Our youngest daughter will soon take over as its head. Our eldest, Sue, had a strong early career in publishing in New York, but left that to start her very successful restaurant, Clementine's, at One Fifth Avenue in Greenwich Village. Dee, our middle child, is a graphic designer in Pasadena.

Jean raised our boys, Marty and Mel, single-highhandedly—though she and I became friends, and I helped where I could. She died of cancer, at the young age of fifty-seven. I was with her the last week of her life. The great statesman Andrew Young delivered her eulogy.

She did a fantastic job with the boys. She gave them love, strong values, and good educations. Marty, who graduated college with a business major, has worked for Motorola in a managerial capacity for over fifteen years. Mel has a Ph.D. in pharmacology and an M.B.A.; he is a Lieutenant

Commander in the U. S. Navy, chief of contingency planning and industrial preparedness in medical readiness. Recently, he was transferred to the Washington, D.C. Naval Headquarters, and a promotion to full-fledged Commander is forthcoming. He and his lovely wife, Moneez, have two beautiful girls, Ryann, ten, and Evan, five.

In the long run, I had a wonderful professional career. Though racism remains an ugly reality in America to this day, after the 1960s, racial impediments decreased, and my accomplishments under Bill Van Ness had already solidified my reputation in the company. Altogether, except for my misbegotten sojourn in the Philippines, I basically spent my entire forty-year career with the same outfit—eight years with Bechtel and thirty-two with the Ralph M. Parsons Company after Bechtel and Parsons split. After I returned from Germany, I did projects for Parsons in California, Texas, Louisiana, Mississippi, New Jersey, Illinois, British Columbia, and Guam—often (successfully) re-taking engineering exams to work in states that did not recognize California licenses.

I am grateful for my career with Parsons. To this day I meet with my old colleagues for lunch every Thursday, with young structural engineers every other week, and with various retired employees groups several times a year. Unfortunately, my retirement came in sad circumstances. Parsons is an employee-owned business, and employees can cash out their shares upon retirement. In 1991, several of us were preparing to retire. However, Parsons had such a profitable year that we decided to put off retirement until after the annual stock re-evaluation. We expected the stock value to rise at least three dollars per share—about twelve percent—given what we knew of the year we had enjoyed. However, when the valuation was announced on March 1, share valuation went down five or six percent. Hell broke lose. Share valuation, we believed, was being manipulated by the new, younger executives. A lower share value was better for them, for they could buy more shares and the company would have to pay us old-timers less to get rid of us.

About five hundred of us old-timers, from vice presidents and project managers down to peons, formed an association to fight the unfair valuation. As the person with the longest, most illustrious association with the company, I was asked to head the association—everyone knew there was no way Parsons could ever fire me in retaliation.

I led many private and public meetings, and I bargained hard. When the chips were down, though, more than half of the association's members backed out. The executives were not willing to deal, and the employees became fearful of their jobs. I failed to get the valuation changed, since I now had the support of only a minority of the old-timers. I felt so ill-used, abandoned, and angry. Not too much later, I retired.

My mother died in 1968, six months after my marriage to Ute. She never met her granddaughters. My father lived to the ripe old age of ninety-seven, dying in 1975. Kaka Mando came to live in America in 1989, but he died one year later. My sisters Cely and my brother Tommy continue to live happily and well. My little sister, Lourdes, died several years ago.

Mary de Guzman did not really give up hope that we would be together until after I married Ute, I think. When Mary heard that Jean and I had separated, she wanted to come to Los Angeles to see me, but my move to Germany nixed that idea. I did not encourage her to come to Germany, for I knew marriage might still be on her mind. Only after Ute and I were married did Mary marry someone else. Then she and I became friends, as we remain to this day.

My dear friend and protector, the brave Pareng Hiling, became a bodyguard for a politician, Mayor Cuneta of Pasay City. Pareng Hiling died violently, in a shoot-out with hoodlums. Jim Ferrer suffered assassination while serving in Cory Aquino's cabinet, overseeing the local governments of municipalities. Always a stickler for clean government, Jim ran afoul of organized crime when he tried to clean up corruption.

The death of Dr. Gabriel is still part of folklore in Don Galo, and on visits back there, I have heard from people who were not even born then that I was one of the triggermen. That is simply not true; the truth is as I have told it in this book. Over the years, I have once run into Dr. Juan's daughter, Astie, and his son, Pabling. While I would not say they were warm to me, nor would I have expected that, they were cordial and respectful. I believe they know the truth. I felt an extra burden of guilt seeing them, for I knew—from my sons—how hard it is to grow up without a father present.

I have often been asked what happened to our beautiful house in Don Galo. Kaka Mando inherited it, and during his first marriage it was his primary residence. In his second marriage, he spent most of the time in his other house in San Gregorio village. The Don Galo house fell into disrepair. One of Kaka Mando's sons-in-law took the house, in repayment for money owed him. He tore it down and built an apartment complex.

That hurt my heart. The house had plenty of history in it. I would have bought it, had it been made available for sale. The option was never really open; the son-in-law wanted the property to build his apartment complex, and Kaka Mando owed him money. Was I angry? Of course I was—and I still am.

I am very fortunate to have inherited the dining-room table from our old house. I had it shipped to America, and we have it now in our house in Pasadena. Made of Philippine mahogany, its top is one solid piece, two-and-a-half inches thick Ute restored it herself, and it is beautiful. It reminds me of our large, happy family in Don Galo, what a good life we had, and how we always shared it with our friends and neighbors.

I have on my wall a gold-plated replica of the gun I took from Pepe, the kidnapper I overpowered to escape. Underneath it, I have a plaque, saying, "Freedom Day—April 7, 1946." By the time I had the money to get the gold-plated gun, I could not remember the exact day I escaped, so I chose my birthday as the day to commemorate my escape.

I wish I could say that I still have the locket with Stella's picture, the one I recovered from the kidnappers. Sadly, when I was at Stanford, I had my most prized possessions—including my grandfather's diamond cuff links and four diamond buttons used for a man's formal shirt in the

Philippines—in a little box, and the box was stolen. I accosted the person I believed was the thief, telling him he could keep the diamonds if he returned the locket. He fiercely denied my accusations, and I never saw the locket again.

I live now high on a hill in Pasadena, a few minutes from the Rose Bowl, where I go walking several times a week, with other people of all ages and nationalities, to stay in shape. Our house overlooks the Rose Bowl, so from our wooded, almost bucolic home, we can watch fireworks on the Fourth of July and after big ball games.

Sometimes when I sit beside our lovely swimming pool watching the automatic sprinkler system nourish our one-acre yard, I chuckle to think how different this is from the days in Paranaque, when we lacked running water and swam in the river. I am very glad, though, that my home today resembles Don Galo in one respect: We hear birds every morning, and we watch deer and rabbits and coyote and other wildlife from the ravine below us come up to feed, and we enjoy the rich shade from many large trees. Ute grows beautiful roses, and I raise exotic fish in a couple of decorative ponds. This part is not so terribly far from my native paradise.

I still love cars—I still have a Porsche, as well as my wife's Saab and a few other sporty vehicles. I still love to dance. I go to the Pasadena Ballroom Dance Club for "Sizzling Salsa—Mambo!" two nights a week and "East Coast Swing," also known as Jitterbug, two other nights. I still love sports, though my playing days are over.

After I left Manila in 1951, I heard, read, and witnessed the resurgence of our country. The Philippines had suffered during the World War II, but we recovered well, until Marcos took over in 1965. We were building one of the best economies in the Far East—but look where we are now!

In my visits home after Marcos was toppled, I have seen how poor we have become. Unemployment is high, yet finding a plumber or an electrician is nearly impossible. Bright young people leave as fast as they can to work abroad. The government has yet to do much to train young people in useful trades. The standard of living has gone down, way down.

Both Don Galo and Paranaque have changed so much that they do not resemble my boyhood home. Back then, Paranaque was really a country town, just a few hundred people surrounded by fields and jungles. Now, it is part and parcel of the Manila sprawl, an urban and suburban place. All the fields and jungles are gone, replaced by everything from nice housing villages, like B.F. Homes and Modern Living, to slum areas to heartbreaking shanty towns.

With so many Filipinos—over two hundred from Don Galo alone—now in the United States, I saw the possibility of helping Don Galo. I formed the Don Galo Association of America. We had all left Don Galo, the place of our birth, in search of greener pastures. We found pastures greener than we had dared dream. Sharing this bounty with the people we left behind is the focus of our group.

We have raised money for Don Galo's daycare center and elementary school. Current plans include a multi-purpose building to be donated to the people of Don Galo, to be used as a community center, where children of all ages can study, where trades will be taught, where seniors will have a place to gather and enjoy each other.

In this surprisingly life, many dreams have come true, and many wonderful things I could never have dreamed have been mine.

Six decades ago, as an adolescent hearing of Pearl Harbor, I could never have predicted the course of my life. I never planned to leave the Philippines forever—even when I dreamed of America, I never thought I would not return to live in my homeland someday. I never expected to travel the world. I never predicted that two of my children would be scions of one of America's greatest families, heirs to a legacy of heroism in the battle for civil rights. I never have expected to marry a beautiful German woman with whom I would have and raise three lovely California girls. I never envisioned a career of designing and building advanced structures all over Europe and America.

Even now, though, especially when I hear the lyric strains of Franz Schubert's *Serenade*, I sometimes shed a tear for Stella. No memory remains more lively, no pain more profound. Her loss remains a defining moment of my life. As I have built the life of my choosing, though, I have gained the freedom to own that memory without destroying myself and those I love. There is room in my life for memory, for my life is one I love. Yes, life with Stella would have been good—but life with Ute has been marvelous. I have sadness for Stella, but no regrets for the life I have had. I have been blessed.

About the Author

Rudy de Lara, born in the Philippine barrio of Don Galo in 1924, served in the guerrilla resistance to the Japanese during World War II. After the war, he was kidnapped for ransom, charged with the murder of his town's mayor, and burdened with the death of his fiancee, all before making his way to America. He earned his Masters degree in engineering from Stanford, became a professional engineer, and for forty years oversaw projects around the globe for Bechtel and The Ralph M. Parsons Company. He became an American citizen over four decades ago. Now retired, he lives in Pasadena with his wife, Ute.

Bob Fancher, the author of *Cultures of Healing: Correcting the Image of American Mental Health Care* and collaborator on many other projects, earned his Ph.D. in philosophy before going on to train as a psychotherapist in New York City. After practicing psychotherapy for fourteen years, he closed up shop to follow the career trajectory of his wife, Melena. He now lives in Austin, Texas, where he writes full-time and Melena programs computers.

9 780595 148066

Printed in Great Britain
by Amazon.co.uk, Ltd.,
Marston Gate.